ExpressWays

Second Edition

428.34
MOL

Steven J. Molinsky
Bill Bliss

PRENTICE HALL REGENTS
A VIACOM COMPANY

Upper Saddle River, NJ 07458

Contributing Author
Ann Kennedy

Molinsky, Steven J.
    ExpressWays 3 / Steven J. Molinsky, Bill Bliss. – – 2nd ed.
      p.   cm.
    Includes index.
    ISBN 0-13-385535-X. (soft cover: alk. paper)
    1. English language– –Textbooks for foreign speakers.   I. Bliss,
Bill. II. Title.
PE1128.M6753   1996
428.2'4– –dc20   95-44120
                                      CIP

Publisher: *Tina Carver*
Director of Production: *Aliza Greenblatt*
Executive Managing Editor: *Dominick Mosco*
Production Supervision/Compositor: *Janice Sivertsen*
Composition Support: *Christine Mann/ Steven Greydanus*
Editorial Supervision: *Janet Johnston*
Production Assistant: *Jennifer Rella*
Manufacturing Manager: *Ray Keating*

Electronic Image Production Supervisor: *Todd Ware*
Electronic Image Production/Scanning: *Marita Froimson*
Electronic Art: *Don Kilcoyne/Marita Froimson/Jan Sivertsen*
Art Director: *Merle Krumper*
Interior Design: *PC&F/Wanda España*
Photographer: *Paul Tañedo*

Illustrator: *Richard Hill*

© 1996 by PRENTICE HALL REGENTS
Prentice-Hall, Inc.
A Simon & Schuster Company
Upper Saddle River, New Jersey 07458

Printed in the United States of America

10 9 8 7 6 5 4 3 2 1

ISBN   0-13-385535-X

Prentice-Hall International (UK) Limited, *London*
Prentice-Hall of Australia Pty. Limited, *Sydney*
Prentice-Hall Canada Inc., *Toronto*
Prentice-Hall Hispanoamericana, S.A., *Mexico*
Prentice-Hall of India Private Limited, *New Delhi*
Prentice-Hall of Japan, Inc., *Tokyo*
Simon & Schuster Asia Pte. Ltd., *Singapore*
Editora Prentice-Hall do Brasil, Ltda., *Rio de Janeiro*

EXPRESSWAYS 3 TRAVEL GUIDE

EXIT 3 • People and Places 35

EXIT 6 • Health and Emergencies

EXIT 7 • Shopping 115

EXIT 8 • Recreation 133

APPENDIX 155

ExpressWays is a comprehensive 4-level course for learners of English. Its innovative spiraled curriculum integrates lifeskill topics, functions, and grammar in an imaginative highway theme that puts students *in the fast lane* for an exciting and motivating journey to English language proficiency.

The program consists of the following components:

- **Student Texts** — offering speaking, reading, writing, and listening comprehension practice that integrates grammar and functions in a topic-based curriculum.

- **Activity Workbooks** — offering reinforcement through grammar, reading, writing, and listening comprehension practice fully coordinated with the student texts. The activity workbooks also feature dynamic exercises in pronunciation, rhythm, stress, and intonation.

- *Navigator* **Companion Books** — visually exciting "magazine-style" texts, offering a complete lifeskill curriculum fully integrated with the *ExpressWays* student texts.

- **Teacher's Guides** — providing background notes and expansion activities for all lessons and step-by-step instructions for teachers.

- **Audio Program** — offering realistic presentations of conversations, listening comprehension exercises, and readings from the student texts and workbooks.

- **Picture Program** — featuring Picture Cards for vocabulary development, enrichment exercises, and role-playing activities.

- **Placement and Achievement Testing Program** — providing tools for the evaluation of student levels and progress.

The *ExpressWays* series is organized by a spiraled curriculum that is covered at different degrees of intensity and depth at each level. *ExpressWays 1* and *2* provide beginning-level students with the most important vocabulary, grammar, and functional expressions needed to communicate at a basic level in a full range of situations and contexts. *ExpressWays 3* and *4* cover the same full range of situations and contexts, but offer intermediate-level students expanded vocabulary, more complex grammar, and a wider choice of functional expressions.

The Dimensions of Communication: Function, Form, and Content

ExpressWays provides dynamic, communicative practice that involves students in lively interactions based on the content of real-life contexts and situations. Every lesson offers students simultaneous practice with one or more functions, the grammatical forms needed to express those functions competently, and the contexts and situations in which the functions and grammar are used. This "tri-dimensional" clustering of function, form, and content is the organizing principle behind each lesson and the cornerstone of the *ExpressWays* approach to functional syllabus design.

ExpressWays offers students broad exposure to uses of language in a variety of relevant contexts: in community, school, employment, home, and social settings. The series gives students practice using a variety of registers, from the formal language someone might use in a job interview, with a customer, or when speaking to an authority figure, to the informal language someone would use when talking with family members, co-workers, or friends.

A special feature of the course is the treatment of discourse strategies — initiating conversations and topics, hesitating, asking for clarification, and other conversation skills.

An Overview

Chapter-Opening Photos

Each chapter-opening page features two photographs of situations that depict key topics presented in the chapter. Students make predictions about who the people are and what they might be saying to each other. In this way, students have the opportunity to share what they already know and to relate the chapter's content to their own lives and experiences.

Guided Conversations

Guided conversations are the dialogs and exercises that are the central learning devices in *ExpressWays*. Each lesson begins with a model conversation that depicts a real-life situation and the vocabulary, grammar, and functions used in the communication exchange. Key functional expressions in the models are in boldface type and are footnoted, referring students to short lists of alternative expressions for accomplishing the functions. In the exercises that follow, students create new conversations by placing new content into the framework of the model, and by using any of the alternative functional expressions.

Original Student Conversations

Each lesson ends with an open-ended exercise that offers students the opportunity to create and present original conversations based on the theme of the lesson. Students contribute content based on their experiences, ideas, and imaginations.

Follow-Up Exercises and Activities

A variety of follow-up exercises and activities reinforce and build upon the topics, functions, and grammar presented in the guided conversation lessons.

- **Constructions Ahead!** exercises provide focused practice with grammar structures.

- **CrossTalk** activities provide opportunities for students to relate lesson content to their own lives.

- **InterActions** activities provide opportunities for role-playing and cooperative learning.

- **Interview** activities encourage students to interview each other as well as people in the community.

- **Community Connections** activities provide task-based homework for students to get out into their communities to practice their language skills.

- **Cultural Intersections** activities offer rich opportunities for cross-cultural comparison.

- **Figure It Out!** activities offer opportunities for problem-solving.

- **Your Turn** activities provide opportunities for writing and discussion of issues presented in the chapter.

- **Listening Exercises** give students intensive listening practice that focuses on functional communication.

- **Reflections** activities provide frequent opportunities for self-assessment, critical thinking, and problem-solving.

- **Reading** passages in every chapter are designed to provide interesting and stimulating content for class discussion. These selections are also available on the accompanying audiotapes for additional listening comprehension practice.

InterChange

This end-of-chapter activity offers students the opportunity to create and present "guided role plays." Each activity consists of a model that students can practice and then use as a basis for their original presentations. Students should be encouraged to be inventive and to use new vocabulary in these presentations and should feel free to adapt and expand the model any way they wish.

Rest Stop

These "free role plays" appear after every few chapters, offering review and synthesis of the topics, functions, and grammar of the preceding chapters. Students are presented with eight scenes depicting conversations between people in various situations. The students determine who the people are and what they are talking about, and then improvise based on their perceptions of the scenes' characters, contexts, and situations. These improvisations promote students' absorption of the preceding chapters' functions and grammar into their repertoire of active language use.

Support and Reference Sections

End-of-Chapter Summaries include the following:

- **Looking Back** — a listing of key functional expressions in the chapter for review.

- **Construction Sign** — a listing of the key grammar structures presented in the chapter.

- **ExpressWays Checklist** — a self-assessment listing of key lifeskills presented in the chapter.

An **Appendix** provides charts of the grammar constructions presented in each chapter, along with a list of cardinal numbers, ordinal numbers, and irregular verbs.

An **Index** provides a convenient reference for locating topics and grammar in the text.

Suggested Teaching Strategies

We encourage you, in using *ExpressWays*, to develop approaches and strategies that are compatible with your own teaching syle and the needs and abilities of your students. While the program does not require any specific method or technique in order to be used effectively, you may find it helpful to review and try out some of the following suggestions. (Specific step-by-step instructions may be found in the *ExpressWays* Teacher's Guides.)

Chapter-Opening Photos

Have students talk about the people and the situations and, as a class or in pairs, predict what the characters might be saying to each other. Students in pairs or small groups may enjoy practicing role plays based on these scenes and then presenting them to the class.

Guided Conversations

1. SETTING THE SCENE: Have students look at the model illustration in the book. Set the scene: Who are the people? What is the situation?

2. LISTENING: With books closed, have students listen to the model conversation — presented by you, by a pair of students, or on the audiotape.

3. CLASS PRACTICE: With books still closed, model each line and have the whole class practice in unison.

4. READING: With books open, have students follow along as two students present the model.

5. PAIR PRACTICE: In pairs, have students practice the model conversation.

6. ALTERNATIVE EXPRESSIONS: Present to the class each sentence of the dialog containing a footnoted expression. Call on different students to present the same sentence, replacing the footnoted expression with its alternatives. (You can cue students to do this quickly by asking, "What's another way of saying that?" or "How else could he/she/you say that?")

7. EXERCISE PRACTICE: (optional) Have pairs of students simultaneously practice all the exercises, using the footnoted expressions or any of their alternatives

8. EXERCISE PRESENTATIONS: Call on pairs of students to present the exercises, using the footnoted expressions or any of their alternatives.

Original Student Conversations

In these activities, which follow the guided conversations at the end of each lesson, have students create and present original conversations based on the theme of the lesson. Encourage students to be inventive as they create their characters and situations. (You may ask students to prepare their original conversations as homework, then practice them the next day with another student and present them to the class. In this way, students can review the previous day's lesson without actually having to repeat the specific exercises already covered.)

CrossTalk

Have students first work in pairs and then share with the class what they talked about.

InterActions

Have pairs of students practice role playing the activity and then present their role plays to the class.

InterView

Have students circulate around the room to conduct their interviews, or have students interview people outside the class. Students should then report to the class about their interviews.

Community Connections

Have students do the activity individually, in pairs, or in small groups and then report to the class.

Cultural Intersections

Have students do the activity in class, in pairs, or in small groups.

Reflections

Have students discuss the questions in pairs or small groups, and then share their ideas with the class.

Your Turn

This activity is designed for both writing practice and discussion. Have students discuss the activity as a class, in pairs, or in small groups. Then have students write their responses at home, share their written work with other students, and discuss in class. Students may enjoy keeping a journal of their written work. If time permits, you may want to write a response to each student's journal, sharing your own opinions and experiences as well as reacting to what the student has written. If you are keeping portfolios of students' work, these compositions serve as excellent examples of students' progress in learning English.

Reading

Have students discuss the topic of the reading beforehand, using the pre-reading questions suggested in the Teacher's Guide. Have students then read the passage silently, or have them listen to the passage and take notes as you read it or play the audiotape.

InterChange

Have students practice the model, using the same steps listed above for guided conversations. Then have pairs of students create and present original conversations, using the model dialog as a guide. Encourage students to be inventive and to use new vocabulary. (You may want to assign this exercise as homework, having students prepare their conversations, practice them the next day with another student, and then present them to the class.) Students should present their conversations without referring to the written text, but they should also not memorize them. Rather, they should feel free to adapt and expand them any way they wish.

Rest Stop

Have students talk about the people and the situations, and then present role plays based on the scenes. Students may refer back to previous lessons as a resource, but they should not simply re-use specific conversations. (You may want to assign these exercises as written homework, having students prepare their conversations, practice them the next day with another student, and then present them to the class.)

We hope that *ExpressWays* offers you and your students a journey to English that is meaningful, effective, and entertaining. Have a nice trip!

Steven J. Molinsky
Bill Bliss

xiv

Components of an ExpressWays Lesson

A **model conversation** offers initial practice with the functions and structures of the lesson.

Key functional expressions are in boldface type and are footnoted, referring students to a box containing alternative expressions for accomplishing the functions.

In the **exercises**, students create new conversations by placing new content into the framework of the model, and by using any of the alternative functional expressions.

The **open-ended exercise** at the end of each lesson asks students to create and present original conversations based on the theme of the lesson.

What's New with You?

A. What's new with you?[1]
B. Nothing much. How about you?
A. Well, actually, I have some good news.
B. Really? What?
A. I just got a big promotion!
B. You did? **That's great!**[2] Congratulations!

[1] What's happening with you?
What's new?
What's happening?

[2] That's wonderful!
That's fantastic!

I just got a big promotion!

1. I just passed my driver's test!
2. My wife had a baby girl last week!
3. My husband and I won the state lottery yesterday!
4. My thirty-two-year-old son finally moved out and found his own apartment!
5. My apple pie won first prize at the county fair last Saturday!

Tell somebody some good news!

20

For example:

Exercise 1 might be completed by placing the new exercise content into the existing model:

A. What's new with you?
B. Nothing much. How about you?
A. Well, actually, I have some good news.
B. Really? What?
A. I just passed my driver's test!
B. You did? That's great! Congratulations!

Exercise 2 might be completed by using the new exercise content and some of the alternative expressions:

A. What's happening with you?
B. Nothing much. How about you?
A. Well, actually, I have some good news.
B. Really? What?
A. My wife had a baby girl last week!
B. She did? That's wonderful! Congratulations!

Sometimes the footnote indicates that an alternative expression requires a change in the grammar of the sentence. For example, the sentences:

| Let's _____! | = | Let's go swimming! |
| Why don't we _____? | = | Why don't we go swimming? |

ExpressWays

Second Edition

3

Exit 1

MEETING AND GREETING PEOPLE GIVING INFORMATION

Take Exit 1 to . . .

➔ Greet someone and introduce yourself, using *wh-questions*

➔ Introduce members of your family

➔ Give information about countries and nationalities

➔ Provide information when checking into a hotel

➔ Provide information at a hospital emergency room

Functions This Exit!

Asking for and Reporting
   Information
Greeting People
Introductions
Initiating Conversations
Correcting

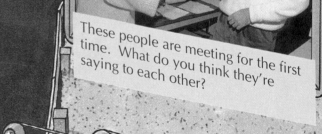

These people are meeting for the first time. What do you think they're saying to each other?

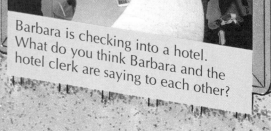

Barbara is checking into a hotel. What do you think Barbara and the hotel clerk are saying to each other?

A. Hello.[1] Let me introduce myself. I'm your neighbor. My name is Linda.

B. Hello.[1] I'm Helen. **Nice to meet you.**[2]

A. **Nice meeting you,**[3] too. Which apartment do you live in?

B. 7A. How about you?

A. 9B.

[1] [*less formal*]
Hi.
[*more formal*]
How do you do?

[2] It's nice to meet you.

[3] It's nice meeting you.

Linda   *Helen*

7A
9B

George   *Miguel*

1 Guatemala
Greece

Bill   *Diane*

2 the 2nd
the 4th

Janet   *Peter*

3 last week
a year ago

Sarah   *Susan*

4 Business
Fine Arts

Frank   *Eddie*

5 I stole* a car.
I robbed a bank.

Greet a new neighbor and introduce yourself.

* steal-stole

2

You're New Here, Aren't You?

A. You're new here, aren't you?

B. Yes, I am. My name is Roger Bell.

A. I'm Jackie Walden. **Nice to meet you.**[1]

B. **Nice meeting you,**[2] too.

A. Tell me, which department do you work in?

B. Personnel. **How about you?**[3]

A. Accounting.

[1] It's nice to meet you.

[2] It's nice meeting you.

[3] What about you?
And you?

Jackie Walden — Personnel

Roger Bell — Accounting

Steve — Don

1 Mr. Crane
Mrs. Benson

Asako — Enku

2 Ethiopia
Japan

Walter — Rose

3 Ms. Wilson's
Mr. Frankel's

Mary — Thelma

4 yesterday
several years ago

Sally — Jimmy

5 It has its "ups and downs."
There are some good days
and some bad days.

Greet someone at work or at school and introduce yourself.

What's the Word?

Who ○ **What** **When** **Where** **Which** **Why** **Whose** ○ **How**

1.
Where do you live?
On the fifth floor.

2.
_____ is she?
She's the new boss.

3.
_____ bank do you go to?
The Empire Bank.

4.
_____ are your parents?
They're fine.

5.
_____ did you start your new job?
Yesterday.

6.
_____ are you majoring in English?
Because I like it.

7.
_____ is your husband's name?
Charles.

8.
_____ book is this?
Maria's.

9.
_____ are you leaving?
In a little while.

10.
_____ is from Greece?
Our whole family.

11.
_____ are you enjoying your new bicycle?
I like it a lot.

12.
_____ do you work?
In Accounting.

4

Constructions Ahead!

Am I?   Is { he / she / it } ?   Are { we / you / they } ?   Do { I / we / you / they } ?   Does { he / she / it } ?

1. Which apartment ___are___ we going to?
2. Where _____ you work?
3. Why _____ I here?
4. What _____ you majoring in?
5. _____ Diane live on the first floor?
6. Who _____ she?
7. _____ we going to be late?
8. _____ you like your new job?

9. When _____ the new tenant going to move in?
10. _____ they from Ecuador?
11. _____ it easy or difficult?
12. How _____ you do?
13. How _____ you?
14. Where _____ your family live?
15. _____ we have to leave now?
16. _____ I going to be okay, Doctor?

Listen

Listen and choose the right answer.

1. a. My brother.
   b. At the bank. *(circled)*

2. a. Elena Fernandez.
   b. Fine.

3. a. To the second floor.
   b. Last week.

4. a. In my car.
   b. To my apartment.

5. a. She's my wife.
   b. She's fine.

6. a. 103.
   b. Last week.

7. a. And you?
   b. English.

8. a. I am.
   b. Nice meeting you.

9. a. Hello.
   b. And you?

More Questions!

1. ____ city are you from?
   a. What *(circled)*
   b. Where

2. ____ class are you in?
   a. Who
   b. Which

3. ____ homework is this?
   a. How
   b. Whose

4. ____ did you start studying?
   a. When
   b. Who

5. ____ is your new neighbor?
   a. Whose
   b. Who

6. ____ did you meet her?
   a. Who
   b. How

7. ____ department is this?
   a. Which
   b. When

8. ____ did you live there?
   a. What
   b. When

9. ____ is your husband?
   a. When
   b. How

5

InterActions

Who do you think these people are? What are they saying to each other? With a partner, create role plays based on these situations and present them to the class.

Cultural Intersections

In the situations on pages 2 and 3, new neighbors, students, and co-workers are meeting for the first time. They greet each other, introduce themselves, and then begin a conversation. People ask questions such as :

> Where are you from?

> Which apartment do you live in?

> Who is your supervisor?

> What floor do you live on?

> When did you start working here?

> Whose class are you in?

> How are you enjoying your work?

In your country, what questions are appropriate to ask someone when you first meet? What questions are inappropriate? Talk with a partner and then share your observations with the class.

Figure It Out!

With a partner, create a scene in which two people meet for the first time. The characters should greet each other, introduce themselves, and then begin a conversation.

Present your scenes to the class, but don't tell what the relationship is and where the conversation is taking place. The rest of the class must guess, based on the questions you ask in your conversations.

> Are you neighbors?
> Are you students in a class?
> Are you at a party?
> Are you waiting together at a doctor's office?

Fill It In!

Fill in the correct word.

A. Excuse me. _____Is_____ [1] this Room 15?

B. Yes, it _____ [2]. _____ [3] you looking for Mr. Bank's class?

A. Yes, I _____ [4].

B. Well, this _____ [5] his room. _____ [6] you in Mr. Bank's class?

A. Yes, I _____ [7]. How about you?

B. _____ [8] in his class, too. By the way, my name _____ [9] Kenji.

A. Hi. _____ [10] Denise. Tell me, what do you know about Mr. Bank? _____ [11] he give a lot of homework?

B. Yes, he _____ [12]. And his tests _____ [13] very hard. Everybody says so.

A. _____ [14] you sure?

B. _____ [15] positive!

Matching Lines

_c_ **1** What floor is your class on?		a. Last week.
____ **2** When did you write to her?		b. I don't think so.
____ **3** Do you have to work this weekend?		c. The second.
____ **4** Where does he come from?		d. Yes. In Toronto.
____ **5** Who do they work for?		e. Mr. Wu.
____ **6** Is Jenny living in Canada?		f. Venezuela.
____ **7** Whose car is this?		g. Fantastic!
____ **8** How's your new motorcycle?		h. Mrs. Morimoto.
____ **9** Who's working late tonight?		i. Alberto's.

A. Hi! How are you?[1]

B. Fine.[2] And you?

A. Fine,[2] thanks. **I'd like to introduce you to**[3] my wife, Patty.

B. Nice to meet you.

[1] *[less formal]*
How are you doing?
How are things?

[2] Good.
All right.

[3] I'd like to introduce
Let me introduce you to
Let me introduce
I'd like you to meet
[less formal]
This is

my wife, Patty

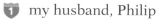

1 my husband, Philip

2 my brother, Carl

3 my daughter, Claudia

4 my father, Mr. Lee

5 my new mother-in-law, Mrs. Walton

Introduce someone to another person.

8

Fill It In!

Fill in the correct answer.

1 How are you ____?
   a. things
   b. doing ⓑ

2 This is ____.
   a. myself
   b. my wife

3 I'd like to ____ myself.
   a. introduce
   b. meet

4 I'm ____.
   a. thank you
   b. all right

5 I'd like to ____ you to Bob.
   a. introduce
   b. meet

6 It's nice to ____ you.
   a. meeting
   b. meet

Meet My Family!

brother   father   mother   niece   son
daughter   husband   nephew   sister   wife

Hello. My name is Ron. I'd like to introduce my family. This is my ___wife___¹, Susan. We have two children, a _____², Michael, and a _____³, Julie.

And these are my parents — my _____⁴, Helen, and my _____⁵, Robert. Also, meet my _____⁶, Tom, and my _____⁷, Elizabeth. Tom isn't married, but Elizabeth is. This is her _____⁸, Jason, and her two children — my _____⁹, Eric, and my _____¹⁰, Janet. I have a wonderful family! Now tell me about yours!

Your Turn

For Writing and Discussion

Tell about members of your family.

What are their names? How old are they? Where do they work or go to school?

Bring in photographs of your family and share your family descriptions with the class.

A. Passport, please!

B. Here you are.

A. *Italian*?

B. Yes.

A. Where in *Italy* are you from?

B. *Florence*.

A. There sure are a lot of people from *Italy* visiting right now.

B. I'm not surprised. Our school year just ended, and a lot of *Italians* are on vacation.

A. How long do you plan to stay?

B. About ten days.

A. All right. Here's your passport. Welcome to *the United States*.

B. Thank you.

A. Next!

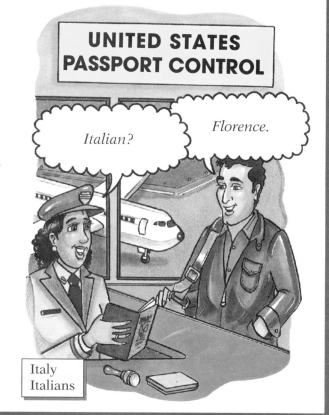

UNITED STATES PASSPORT CONTROL

Italian?

Florence.

Italy
Italians

CANADA PASSPORT CONTROL

Swedish?

Stockholm.

AUSTRALIA PASSPORT CONTROL

Japanese?

Tokyo.

UNITED KINGDOM PASSPORT CONTROL

Spanish?

Barcelona.

1 Sweden
Swedes

2 Japan
Japanese

3 Spain
Spaniards

NEW ZEALAND PASSPORT CONTROL

Korean?

Seoul.

UNITED STATES PASSPORT CONTROL

Brazilian?

Rio de Janeiro.

Go through customs!

4 Korea
Koreans

5 Brazil
Brazilians

ExpressWays

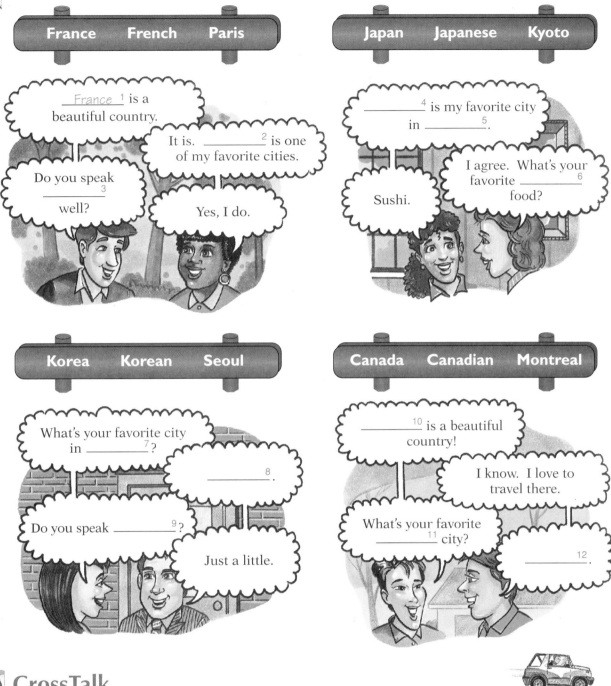

France   French   Paris

___France___ ¹ is a beautiful country.

It is. _____ ² is one of my favorite cities.

Do you speak _____ ³ well?

Yes, I do.

Japan   Japanese   Kyoto

_____ ⁴ is my favorite city in _____ ⁵.

I agree. What's your favorite _____ ⁶ food?

Sushi.

Korea   Korean   Seoul

What's your favorite city in _____ ⁷?

_____ ⁸.

Do you speak _____ ⁹?

Just a little.

Canada   Canadian   Montreal

_____ ¹⁰ is a beautiful country!

I know. I love to travel there.

What's your favorite _____ ¹¹ city?

_____ ¹².

CrossTalk

With a partner, complete the following any way you wish and present your conversations to the class.

A. What country are you going to on your vacation?
B. . . . .
A. What's your favorite . . . . food?
B. . . . .
A. Tell me, do you speak . . . . ?
B. (Yes, I do. / No, I don't.) How about you? Where are YOU going to go on your vacation?

I Have a Reservation

A. May I help you?

B. Yes. I have a reservation.

A. What's your last name?

B. Francovich.

A. **Could you spell that, please?**[1]

B. F-R-A-N-C-O-V-I-C-H.

A. First name Thomas?

B. **That's right.**[2]

A. I see here you requested twin beds.

B. **No, actually not.**[3] I requested a king-size bed.

[1] Could you please spell that?

[2] That's correct.

[3] Not really.

You requested twin beds.

a king-size bed

Thomas Francovich

You're staying 3 nights.

2 nights

Bruce Holmes

You requested a suite.

a regular room

Emily Creighton

You're traveling with your family.

alone

Henry Sanchez

You asked for a room facing the street.

facing the park

Michael Tillman

You're charging your bill to your American Express card.

paying by check

Elizabeth Knowlton

Check into a hotel!

Crossed Lines

Put the following lines in the correct order.

____ No. I'm afraid not.

____ Andersen.

____ No, actually not. I requested a non-smoking room. I'm allergic to smoke.

__1__ May I help you?

____ You don't?!

____ Is your first name Ingrid?

____ Yes. I have a reservation.

____ I'm afraid we don't have any non-smoking rooms.

____ Could you please spell that?

____ What's your last name?

____ A-N-D-E-R-S-E-N.

____ I see here you requested a smoking room.

____ That's correct.

InterActions

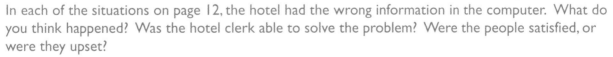

In each of the situations on page 12, the hotel had the wrong information in the computer. What do you think happened? Was the hotel clerk able to solve the problem? Were the people satisfied, or were they upset?

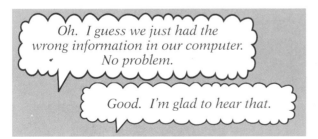

Oh. I guess we just had the wrong information in our computer. No problem.

Good. I'm glad to hear that.

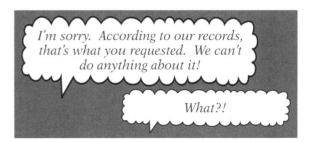

I'm sorry. According to our records, that's what you requested. We can't do anything about it!

What?!

With a partner, choose one of the situations and continue the scene any way you wish. Present your role plays to the class and compare the "happy" and "unhappy" endings to each of these situations.

INTERCHANGE

We Need Some Information

A. Before you can see a doctor, we need some information.

B. Okay.

A. What's your last name?

B. *Prator*.

A. Could you spell that, please?

B. *P-R-A-T-O-R.*

A. And your first name?

B. *Charles*.

A. Address?

B. *35 Winter Street in Middletown.*

A. Telephone number?

B. *732-4495.*

A. What's your date of birth?

B. *May 15th, 1975.*

A. Occupation?

B. *Shoe salesman.*

A. What's your Social Security number?

B. I'm sorry. I don't remember.

A. Do you have medical insurance?

B. Yes, I do. *Blue Cross/Blue Shield.*

A. Do you know your I.D. number?

B. I'm afraid not. I left my membership card at home.

A. That's okay. Take a seat over there, and somebody will see you in a few minutes.

You hurt yourself! You're at the emergency room and want to see a doctor, but first you have to provide some information. Create an original conversation, using the model dialog above as a guide. Feel free to adapt and expand the model any way you wish.

REFLECTIONS
Think of all the companies and offices that have personal information about you. What kind of information do they have? How do they use it? What's your opinion about this?

Discuss in pairs or small groups, and then share your ideas with the class.

InterActions

Complete the missing lines in the following situation and act it out with a partner.

May I help you?

Yes. Is this the Personnel Office?

Yes, it is.

I'm a new employee.

What's your name? 1?

Armando Martinez.

Nice to meet you, Mr. Martinez. Let me fill out this *New Employee Form*. _____ 2?

M-A-R-T-I-N-E-Z.

_____ 3?

694 Crane Drive.

_____ 4?

559-7854.

_____ 5?

My Social Security number is 045-67-8932.

_____ 6?

No. I don't have medical insurance.

_____ 7?

My supervisor's name is Mrs. Kitano.

Okay. Thank you very much, Mr. Martinez. I'm glad you're going to be working with us.

I am, too.

Reading: *No More Numbers, Please!*

Maria came to the United States from Mexico a few days ago. She's staying with her brother and his family all summer because she wants to study English at the local university.

Maria had to fill out a long form at the university. She was very surprised because she had to remember so many numbers. She wrote her brother's address with the zip code and apartment number, her new telephone number and area code, her passport number, and her brother's office telephone number. The form also asked for a Social Security number and a medical insurance I.D. number, but she didn't have those.

Maria gave the form to the secretary in the English Department. The secretary took the form and said, "Write this number down. Don't forget it. It's your student I.D. number, and it's very important. Please put this number on your check when you pay your tuition, and put it under your name whenever you take tests. You'll also need this number to take books out of the library." Another number to remember! Maria wrote down the long number: 90X31058.

Maria had a headache and wanted to go home. She remembered that the Number 93 bus came at 10:11. Or was it the Number 39 bus at 11:10? Oh, no! Too many numbers!

Do You Remember?

Try to answer these questions without looking back at the reading.

1 Maria is _____.
   a. a student
   b. a secretary
   c. English

2 Maria is going to study _____.
   a. her Social Security number
   b. Spanish
   c. during the summer

3 She's staying _____.
   a. at the university
   b. in Mexico
   c. with her brother

4 On the form, Maria wrote _____.
   a. her address in Mexico
   b. her office telephone number
   c. her address in the United States

5 She also wrote _____.
   a. her Social Security number
   b. her passport number
   c. her medical insurance number

6 The number 90X31058 is _____.
   a. her Social Security number
   b. her student I.D. number
   c. the bus number

7 Maria had a headache because _____.
   a. she wanted to go home
   b. she remembered that the Number 93 bus comes at 10:11
   c. she had to remember too many numbers

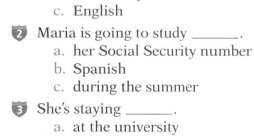

16

Yes, No, or Maybe?

1. Maria came to the United States because she wanted to study English.
2. Maria's brother and his family live in Mexico.
3. Maria's parents live in Mexico.
4. Maria's brother lives in an apartment building.
5. Maria filled in her Social Security number on the university form.
6. The secretary in the English Department wasn't very pleasant.
7. A zip code is part of a telephone number.
8. Maria didn't rememer the number of her bus.
9. She remembered the time of her bus.
10. Maria has trouble remembering a lot of numbers.

Matching Numbers

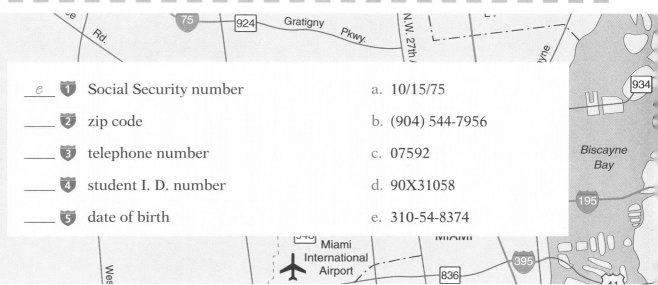

_e_ 1	Social Security number	a. 10/15/75
___ 2	zip code	b. (904) 544-7956
___ 3	telephone number	c. 07592
___ 4	student I. D. number	d. 90X31058
___ 5	date of birth	e. 310-54-8374

Figure It Out!

Make a list of all the numbers in your life — for example, your telephone number, license number, Social Security number, passport number, zip code, area code, telephone number, street number, apartment number, medical insurance number.

Say a number and see if others in the class can guess what the number is.

07634

your zip code

☐ **Greeting People**

Hello
[less formal]
Hi
[more formal]
How do you do?

Nice to meet you.
It's nice to meet you.
Nice meeting you.
It's nice meeting you.

How are you?
[less formal]
How are you doing?
How are things?
  Fine.
  Good.
  All right.

☐ **Introductions**

I'd like to introduce you to _____.
I'd like to introduce _____.
Let me introduce you to _____.
Let me introduce _____.
I'd like you to meet _____.
[less formal]
This is _____.

☐ **Asking for and Reporting Information**

I'm _____.
My name is _____.

Could you spell that, please?
Could you please spell that?

What about you?
And you?

☐ **Correcting**

No, actually not.
Not really.

Now Leaving Exit 1 Construction Area

☐ **Tense Review**
☐ **Question Formation**
☐ **WH-Questions**

Sorry for the inconvenience. For more information see pages 156 and 157.

ExpressWays Checklist

I can . . .

☐ greet someone and introduce myself

☐ introduce members of my family

☐ give information about country and nationality at customs

☐ provide information when checking into a hotel

☐ provide information at a hospital emergency room

SHARING NEWS AND INFORMATION

Take Exit 2 to . . .

➤ Tell about past events, using the past tense

➤ Talk about events with friends, neighbors, and co-workers, using different verb tenses

➤ Tell about weekend plans, using *going to* and *will*

➤ Tell about yourself and your family, using different verb tenses

Functions This Exit!

Asking for and Reporting Information
Congratulating
Sympathizing
Intention
Initiating a Conversation
Certainty/Uncertainty
Probability/Improbability

Alex is telling Martin some news. Is it good news, or is it bad news? What do you think they're saying to each other?

Brenda is telling Roland about something she just heard. What do you think they're saying to each other?

A. What's new with you?[1]

B. Nothing much. How about you?

A. Well, actually, I have some good news.

B. Really? What?

A. I just got a big promotion!

B. You did? **That's great!**[2] Congratulations!

> [1] What's happening with you?
> What's new?
> What's happening?
>
> [2] That's wonderful!
> That's fantastic!

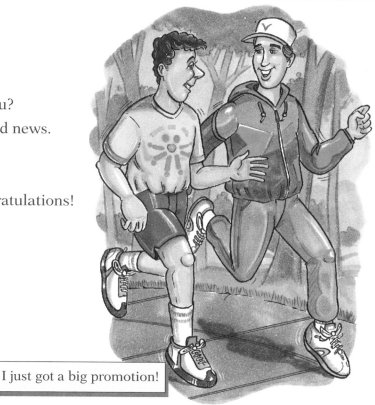

I just got a big promotion!

1 I just passed my driver's test!

2 My wife had a baby girl last week!

3 My husband and I won the state lottery yesterday!

4 My thirty-two-year-old son finally moved out and found* his own apartment!

5 My apple pie won first prize at the county fair last Saturday!

Tell somebody some good news!

* find-found

20

ExpressWays

get-got ○ win-won find-found give-gave ○ leave-left

1
What's happening?

I ___left___ my keys in my apartment. Now I can't get in!

2
What's new with you?

I just _____ a raise!

3
So what's new?

My wife and I finally _____ an apartment.

4
What's happening with you?

The people at the office _____ me a surprise birthday party!

5
So what's new with you?

I _____ the lottery the other day!

6
So what's happening?

Timmy _____ his lunch at home. I have to take it to him at school.

CrossTalk

Think of occasions when you congratulate people—for example, when someone has a baby, graduates from school, gets engaged, gets a promotion, or passes an important exam in school. How do you express your congratulations?

Do you send a card? Do you send a gift?
Do you take the person out to a restaurant?
Do you have a special party for the person?

Talk with a partner, and then share your personal experiences with the class.

A. You seem upset. Is anything wrong?

B. Yes, as a matter of fact, there is.

A. Oh? What?

B. I got a ticket for speeding on my way to work this morning!

A. You did? **That's too bad!**[1] **I'm very sorry to hear that.**[2]

> [1] That's a shame!
> What a shame!
>
> [2] I'm very sorry.
> I'm so sorry.

I got a ticket for speeding on my way to work this morning!

1 My son wrecked the car last night!

2 I didn't get the raise I was hoping for!

3 My daughter broke* up with her fiancé yesterday!

4 All my plants died while I was away on vacation!

5 I didn't receive any Valentine's Day cards this year!

Tell somebody some bad news!

* break-broke

Fill It In!

1. I got a new job, but I __didn't__ __get__ a raise.

2. We didn't buy the blue one. We __bought__ the red one.

3. I found my house keys, but I _____ _____ my car keys.

4. When I was in Washington, I didn't see the president. I _____ the vice-president.

5. Amanda didn't write to her friend Susie. She _____ to her grandparents instead.

6. I ate some ice cream, but I _____ _____ any strawberries. I'm allergic to them.

7. I won a prize at the school fair. I _____ _____ first prize, but that's okay.

8. I didn't go to work today. I _____ to the doctor instead. I didn't feel very well.

9. I'm sorry I _____ _____ Biology. I took Physics instead . . . and I'm flunking the course!

10. I didn't make a cake. I _____ chocolate chip cookies instead. They were delicious!

11. Harry didn't have a good day today. He _____ a bad day. He didn't wake up on time. He _____ up an hour late.

Listen

Listen and choose the most appropriate response.

1. (a.) That's great!
   b. That's a shame!

2. a. That's fantastic!
   b. What a shame!

3. a That's wonderful!
   b. I'm sorry to hear that.

4. a. That's too bad!
   b. Congratulations!

5. a. What a shame!
   b. That's wonderful!

6. a. I'm very sorry.
   b. That's great!

7. a. I'm so sorry.
   b. That's fantastic!

8. a. That's a shame!
   b. That's wonderful!

9. a. That's great!
   b. That's too bad!

Community Connections

Good News or Bad News?

Look in your local newspaper and cut out several headlines. Bring the headlines to class and ask others to decide if the headlines are "good news" or "bad news."

Can I Ask You a Question?

A. Mohammed?

B. Yes?

A. **Can I ask you a question?**¹

B. Sure. What?

A. Is our English teacher going to quit?

B. No. Our English teacher isn't going to quit. **Where did you hear that?**²

A. Some students were talking about it in the hallway.

B. Well, I can't believe it's true. I'm sure it's just a rumor.

¹ Can I ask you something?

² Who told you that?

Some students were talking about it in the hallway.

1 I heard it in the cafeteria.

2 Someone mentioned it at the bus stop.

3 I heard it from the security guard.

4 The whole office is talking about it.

5 I heard it from somebody at the laundromat.

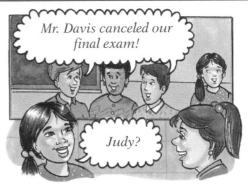

6 Everyone in the class is talking about it.

7 One of the secretaries told me.

8 Some of the girls were talking about it in the locker room.

9 Some people were talking about it at our last union meeting.

10 I overheard a conversation on the elevator.

11 Bobby Rutherford told me.

Rumors

1. _Is Bill going to move to_ California?

No. Bill is going to move to Nevada.

2. _____ last weekend?

No. They got married last month.

3. _____ the secretaries?

No. The boss plans to lay off the managers.

4. _____ on strike?

No. The teachers aren't going to go on strike. It's just a rumor.

5. _____ quit?

No. Alice doesn't want to quit. She wants to take a vacation.

6. _____ our building?

No. The Apex Company bought the building across the street.

7. _____ take a cut in pay?

No. We aren't going to have to take a cut in pay.

8. _____ cancel the final exam?

No. Mr. Miller canceled the school picnic.

More Rumors

1. I _didn't hear_ it from Jan. I heard it from JOHN.

2. The boss _____ Larry. She fired BARRY.

3. We _____ our hours. We have to shorten our BREAKS.

4. They _____ the day shift. They're going to lay off the NIGHT SHIFT.

5. She _____ to Tom. She got married to TIM.

6. They _____ about it in the office. They were talking about it in the ELEVATOR.

7. He _____ leave the company. He just wants to take a vacation.

8. Our supervisor _____ engaged. He's getting a DIVORCE.

9. Between you and me, I'm sure _____ true. I'm sure it's just a rumor.

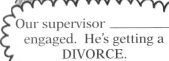

CrossTalk

Start a rumor! Whisper it into the ear of one student. That student whispers it into the ear of another student. Continue around the room until the last student hears the rumor and tells the class. Is the rumor the same one you started with?

A. What are you going to do this weekend?

B. My husband and I are going to repaint our kitchen.

A. Repaint your kitchen?! You're certainly going to be busy!

B. I suppose so. How about you? What are YOUR plans for the weekend?

A. **I'm not sure.**[1] **I'll probably**[2] visit my grandchildren.

B. Well, have a good weekend!

A. You, too.

[1] I don't know for sure.
I'm not positive.

[2] I'll most likely
I'm pretty sure I'll

visit my grandchildren

1 go to the beach

2 see a movie

3 stay home and watch TV

4 work in my garden

5 do some chores around the house

Talk with a friend about your weekend plans.

28

ExpressWays

1 When will you finish your peas, Albert?

    <u>I'll finish</u> them very soon. I promise.

2 Honey, when are you going to write your term paper?

    <u>I'm going to write</u> it this weekend.

3 So when will you tell Bobby the good news?

    _____ him when he gets home.

4 Mrs. Appleton, when will we have to take the cut in pay?

    Unfortunately, _____ the cut in pay next month.

5 When are you and your wife going to see your new grandson?

    _____ him next weekend. We can't wait!

6 Mr. Mudge, when am I going to get a raise?

    _____ a raise very soon.

7 What do you think? How many people will come to our party?

    I'm positive that EVERYBODY _____ to our party!

8 When is your mother going to take us to the circus, Billy?

    _____ us to the circus this Saturday afternoon.

9 So Carlos, where will you be this weekend?

    _____ home doing chores around the house. How about you?

CrossTalk

Talk with a partner about chores you do around the house.

> Which do you enjoy the most? Why?
> Which do you enjoy the least? Why?
> Which chores are you especially _good at_?

Then tell the class about your conversation.

INTERCHANGE

Tell Me a Little About Yourself

A. So, tell me a little about yourself.

B. Gee . . . uh. I don't know where to begin. What do you want to know?

A. Well . . . Are you originally from around here?

B. No, I'm originally from Chicago. I was born there, I grew* up there, and I went to school there. How about you?

A. I was born right here in Los Angeles and lived here until I finished high school. I lived in Denver for several years, and then I moved back here a year ago.

B. Tell me about your family. Do you have any brothers and sisters?

A. Yes. I have a brother and two sisters. They all live in San Diego. How about you?

B. I have a sister. She lives in Cleveland.

A. By the way, what do you do?

B. I'm a journalist. And you?

A. I'm a dentist.

B. A dentist? That's interesting.

A. So, tell me a little about yourself.

B. Gee . . . uh. I don't know where to begin. What do you want to know?

A. Well . . . Are you originally from around here?

B. _____. How about you?

A. _____.

B. Tell me about your family. Do you have any brothers and sisters?

A. _____. How about you?

B. _____.

A. By the way, what do you do?

B. I'm a _____. And you?

A. I'm a _____.

B. A _____? That's interesting.

You're talking to somebody you just met at a party. Create an original conversation, using the model dialog above as a guide. Feel free to adapt and expand the model any way you wish.

* grow-grew

InterView

Be a reporter! Interview a student in your class. Ask the following questions:

Where are you originally from?
Where did you grow up?
Where did you go to school?
Tell about members of your family.
Tell more about yourself.

Write up your interview, combine it with everybody else's, and publish a class magazine containing interviews with all the students in your class.

Listen

Listen and choose the correct answer.

1. a. She's from Los Angeles.
   b. She's from Denver.

2. a. His name is Jim.
   b. He teaches gym.

3. a. They'll both get more money.
   b. They're both going to have rice.

4. a. He's going to take the test.
   b. He took the test.

5. a. They're going to go on strike.
   b. They went on strike.

6. a. They aren't sure about Fred.
   b. Fred is going far away.

7. a. They're in Vancouver.
   b. She went to college in Vancouver.

REFLECTIONS
What kind of person are you—*outgoing* or *shy*? Is it easy or difficult for you to talk with new people you meet? Do you feel comfortable in new situations?

Discuss in pairs or small groups, and then share your ideas with the class.

8. a. He's originally from Taipei.
   b. He went to college in Taipei.

9. a. He wrote for a newspaper.
   b. He taught English.

10. a. She only has one child.
    b. She has a son and a daughter.

Matching Lines

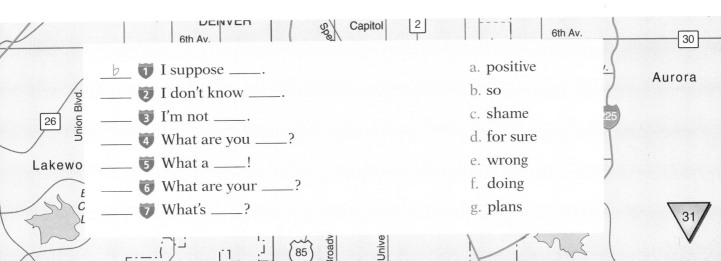

_b_ 1. I suppose ____.	a. positive
____ 2. I don't know ____.	b. so
____ 3. I'm not ____.	c. shame
____ 4. What are you ____?	d. for sure
____ 5. What a ____!	e. wrong
____ 6. What are your ____?	f. doing
____ 7. What's ____?	g. plans

31

Many people look forward to the weekend. It's the time to relax, have fun, and do things around the house.

On Friday nights, many people like to relax after work. They go out for dinner, or they go to movies, concerts, or plays. Other people just like to stay home and watch TV.

On Saturday mornings, supermarkets and shopping malls are crowded with people buying food, clothing, presents, and other things they need.

Many people do chores around the house on Saturday afternoons. They paint, clean attics and basements, rake leaves, do laundry, and wash cars.

On Saturday evenings, many people like to go out. They visit friends, invite people to come over for dinner, or go to a movie, the theater, or a sporting event.

On Sunday mornings, many people like to sleep late, especially people who stayed up late on Saturday night. People often go to church on Sunday. They read the newspaper and often eat a late breakfast called "brunch."

On Sunday afternoons when the weather is nice, many families go to the zoo or to the park. During the winter, many people spend Sunday afternoons at theaters, museums, or shopping malls. Many families have a big dinner on Sunday afternoons. Grandparents and other relatives often come to visit.

On Sunday evenings, people usually stay home and prepare for the week ahead. Weekends can be very busy!

True or False?

1. Weekends begin on Saturday afternoons.

2. People often shop on Saturday mornings.

3. People usually relax on Saturday afternoons.

4. Many people don't stay home on Saturday evenings.

5. People probably eat brunch at around 11:00 in the morning.

6. The zoo is probably crowded on beautiful Sunday afternoons.

7. There are usually a lot of parties on Sunday nights.

Do You Remember?

Try to answer these questions without looking back at the reading.

1. People relax, have fun, and do chores _____.
   a. on Friday nights
   b. during the weekends
   c. on Saturday evenings

2. Most Americans do their shopping _____.
   a. on Friday evenings
   b. on Sunday mornings
   c. on Saturdays

3. People usually spend Sunday afternoons inside _____.
   a. when the weather is cold
   b. during the summer months
   c. and eat brunch

4. Most people look forward to the weekend because _____.
   a. everybody goes shopping
   b. they don't have to go to their jobs
   c. they're very busy

5. On Sunday mornings many people like to _____.
   a. go to a movie
   b. go to church
   c. go to parties

6. People probably go to bed early on _____.
   a. Friday nights
   b. Saturday nights
   c. Sunday nights

Cultural Intersections

Talk with a partner about weekends in your country.

When does the weekend start?
What do people typically do on Friday nights?
What do people do on Saturdays?
What do people do on Sundays?

Is the weekend as important in your country as it is in the United States? Talk with a partner, and then share your thoughts with the class.

Looking Back

☐ **Asking for Information**
What's new with you?
What's happening with you?
What's new?
What's happening?

Where did you hear that?
Who told you that?

☐ **Congratulating**
That's great!
That's wonderful!
That's fantastic!

☐ **Sympathizing**
That's too bad!
That's a shame!
What a shame!

I'm very sorry to hear that.
I'm very sorry.
I'm so sorry.

☐ **Initiating a Conversation**
Can I ask you a question?
Can I ask you something?

☐ **Uncertainty**
I'm not sure.
I don't know for sure.
I'm not positive.

☐ **Probability**
I'll probably _____.
I'll most likely _____.
I'm pretty sure I'll _____.

Now Leaving Exit 2 Construction Area

☐ **Yes/No Questions**
☐ **Negative Sentences**
☐ **Question Formation**
☐ **Past Tense**
☐ **Future: Going to**
☐ **Future: Will**

Sorry for the inconvenience. For more information see pages 158 and 159.

ExpressWays Checklist

I can . . .

☐ tell about past events
☐ talk about events with friends, neighbors, and co-workers
☐ tell about weekend plans
☐ tell about myself and my family

34

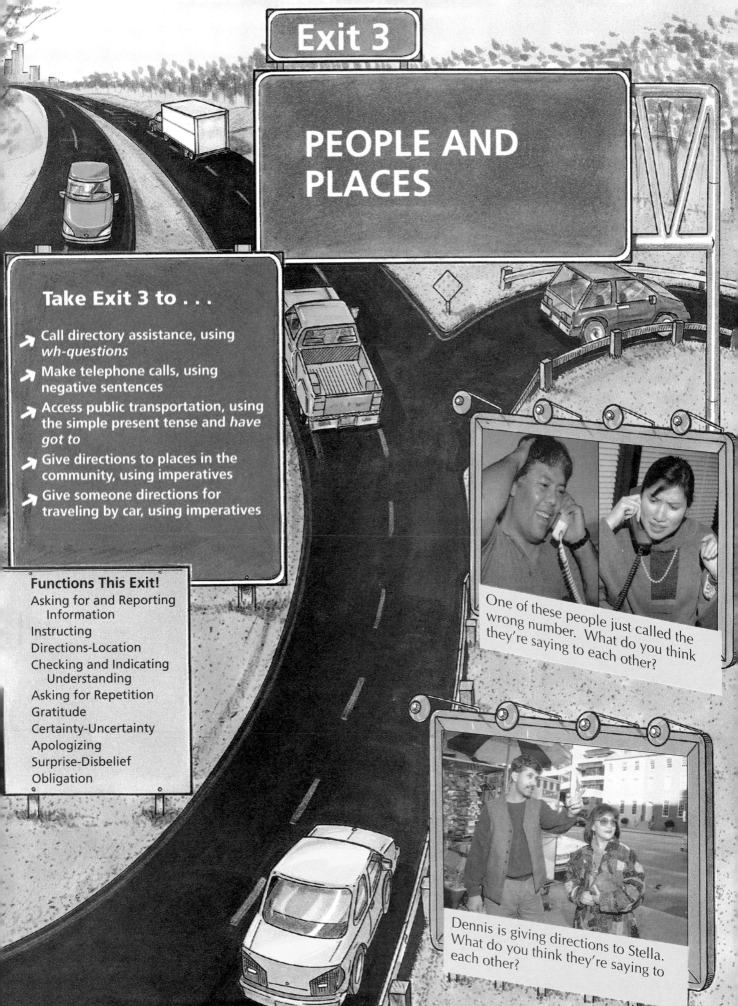

Exit 3

PEOPLE AND PLACES

Take Exit 3 to . . .

→ Call directory assistance, using *wh-questions*

→ Make telephone calls, using negative sentences

→ Access public transportation, using the simple present tense and *have got to*

→ Give directions to places in the community, using imperatives

→ Give someone directions for traveling by car, using imperatives

Functions This Exit!

Asking for and Reporting Information
Instructing
Directions-Location
Checking and Indicating Understanding
Asking for Repetition
Gratitude
Certainty-Uncertainty
Apologizing
Surprise-Disbelief
Obligation

One of these people just called the wrong number. What do you think they're saying to each other?

Dennis is giving directions to Stella. What do you think they're saying to each other?

A. Directory assistance. What city?

B. Miami. I'd like the number of Carlos Ramirez.

A. How do you spell that?[1]

B. R-A-M-I-R-E-Z.

A. What street?

B. Beach Boulevard.

A. Just a moment. . . . I'm sorry, but I don't have a Carlos Ramirez on Beach Boulevard. Are you **sure**[2] you have the correct address?

B. Hmm. **I think so,**[3] but I'd better check. Thank you, Operator.

[1] Can you spell that?

[2] certain
positive

[3] I'm pretty sure,

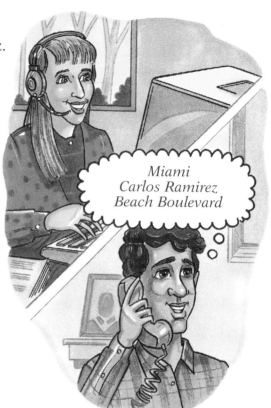

*Miami
Carlos Ramirez
Beach Boulevard*

1
*Cincinnati
Michael Wittler
Madison Road*

2
*Boston
Cathy Flanigan
Dorchester Avenue*

3
*San Francisco
Roberta Yu
Mason Street*

4
*Dallas
Earl Henley
Northwest Highway*

5
*Chicago
Krizick's Auto Repairs
South Shore Drive*

Call directory assistance!

Listen 1

Listen and complete the sentence.

1 a. in Dallas.
b. right now.

2 a. at the red light?
b. in the grocery store?

3 a. try again.
b. are good for you.

4 a. in the envelopes.
b. in the garage.

5 a. to the store.
b. until 6:00.

6 a. class?
b. to the circus?

7 a. in your garden?
b. for the weekend?

8 a. before we cook it.
b. floor.

9 a. to get there?
b. she is?

Listen 2

Listen to the conversation and circle the word you hear.

1 a. You
b. Yu

2 a. Flanigan
b. Flanagin

3 a. Beech
b. Beach

4 a. Whittier
b. Wittler

5 a. Krizick
b. Krizik

6 a. Rio di Janiero
b. Rio de Janeiro

7 a. Hanley
b. Henley

8 a. Ramirez
b. Ramires

Community Connections

Make up a **Personal Telephone Directory** of telephone numbers that you think are important to have—for example: ambulance, fire department, doctor, hospital, clinic, electrician, and plumber. Also include friends and businesses you call often. Either use your local telephone book or call directory assistance to get any numbers you don't already have.

A. Hello.

B. Hello, Joe?

A. I'm sorry. There's nobody here by that name.

B. Is this 965-0231?

A. No, it isn't.

B. Oh. **I apologize.**[1] I guess I dialed the wrong number.

[1] Excuse me.
I'm sorry.

ExpressWays

| isn't | aren't | wasn't | weren't | don't | doesn't | didn't |

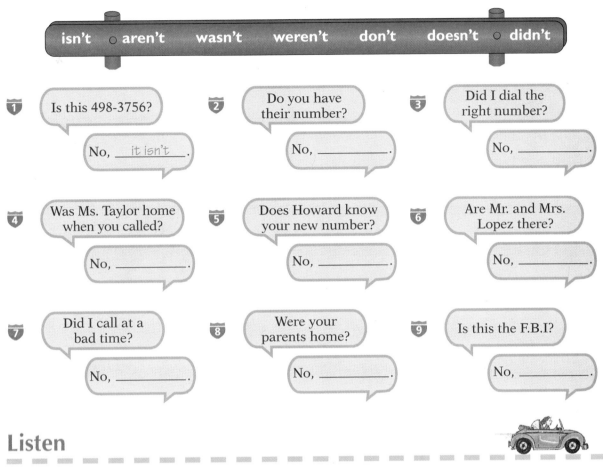

1 Is this 498-3756?

No, __it isn't__.

2 Do you have their number?

No, _____.

3 Did I dial the right number?

No, _____.

4 Was Ms. Taylor home when you called?

No, _____.

5 Does Howard know your new number?

No, _____.

6 Are Mr. and Mrs. Lopez there?

No, _____.

7 Did I call at a bad time?

No, _____.

8 Were your parents home?

No, _____.

9 Is this the F.B.I?

No, _____.

Listen

Listen to the conversation and choose the number you hear.

1 a. 593-7855
(b.) 539-7899

2 a. 952-8622
b. 592-8622

3 a. 832-5600
b. 832-5660

4 a. 860-5439
b. 680-3954

5 a. 438-3593
b. 834-5935

6 a. 648-2341
b. 648-2541

InterActions

With a partner, complete the following telephone conversation any way you wish and then present your conversation to the class. What kinds of "important news" do different students have?

A. Hello.

B. Hello, ... ? This is . . . .
I have something extremely important to tell you.

A. What?

B. . . . .

39

A. Excuse me.[1] Does this train go to the Bronx?

B. No, it doesn't. It goes to Queens. You want the Number 4 train.

A. The Number 4 train?

B. Yes.[2]

A. Where can I get it?

B. It's on track 2.

A. Thank you.[3]

[1] Pardon me.

[2] Uh-húh.
Um-hḿm.
That's right.

[3] Thanks.
Thank you very much.
Thanks very much.

train
the Number 4 train
on track 2

1 bus
the Florida bus
at gate 9

2 train
the Nevada Express
on track 7

3 plane
flight 493
at gate 16

4 ship
The Island Princess
at pier 12

5 monorail
the Orange Monorail
on the other platform

Ask how to get somewhere by bus, train, plane, or boat.

Fill It In!

Fill in the correct answer.

1. Flight 35 leaves from ____ 12.
   a. gate
   b. track

2. You can get your ____ here.
   a. plane
   b. track

3. Your ship leaves from ____ 2.
   a. platform
   b. pier

4. The Number 6 ____ is on track 1.
   a. train
   b. bus

5. The ____ is leaving now.
   a. monorail
   b. platform

6. Your ____ is at gate 13.
   a. bus
   b. pier

7. It goes to the ____.
   a. flight
   b. parking lot

8. Where can I ____ the A train?
   a. go to
   b. get

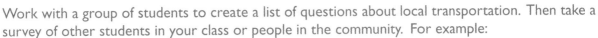

Transportation Survey

Work with a group of students to create a list of questions about local transportation. Then take a survey of other students in your class or people in the community. For example:

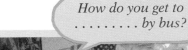

How do you get to
. . . . by bus?

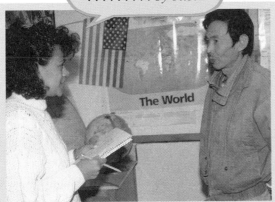

How do you get to
. . . . by train?

If you live in . . . . and
work in . . . . , what's
the best way to get to work?

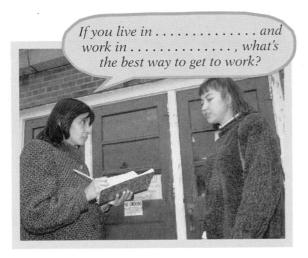

Which airline has the cheapest
flight to . . . . ?

Discuss your results as a group. How did people respond? Did you learn any easier, faster, or cheaper ways to get places?

A. Excuse me. Where can I get the 8:30 flight to Chicago?

B. I'm sorry, but the 8:30 flight to Chicago just left.

A. Oh, no! I missed the flight?!

B. I'm afraid you did.

A. **I don't believe it!** [1] **I've got to** [2] get to my brother's wedding. When is the next flight?

B. **Let me see.** [3] It's at 9:45. Will that get you to Chicago in time for your brother's wedding?

A. I hope so.

> [1] I can't believe it! [3] Let's see.
>
> [2] I have to
>   I need to

my brother's wedding

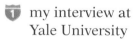 my interview at Yale University

 my high school reunion

 a business meeting

 my nephew's college graduation

 my Aunt Gertrude's funeral

Uh-oh! You just missed your flight, bus, or train! What are you going to do?

Listen

Listen to the announcements. Which words do you hear?

1. a. Las Vegas
   b. Los Angeles

2. a. gate 7
   b. gate 11

3. a. 9:30
   b. 5:30

4. a. Philadelphia
   b. Broadway

5. a. gate 45
   b. gate 17

6. a. San Francisco
   b. San Fernando

7. a. 8:02
   b. 10:30

8. a. 8:00
   b. gate 8

ExpressWays

1. **A.** Excuse me. _Where is the 7:15 train to Philadelphia_ ?
   B. The 7:15 train to Philadelphia is on track 5.
   A. Track 5?
   B. Right.

2. **A.** Pardon me. _____?
   B. The next flight to London is at 6:30.
   A. At 6:30?
   B. Yes. That's correct.

3. **A.** Pardon me. _____?
   B. You can buy a ticket right here.
   A. Right here?
   B. Yes.

4. **A.** Pardon me. _____?
   B. The next ferry to Manhattan leaves at 8:00.
   A. At 8:00?
   B. That's right.

5. **A.** Excuse me. _____?
   B. The flight from Detroit is late because it's snowing there.
   A. It's snowing there?
   B. Yes.

CrossTalk

Think about a time you missed a bus, train, boat, or plane. When was it? Did you miss something important? Talk with a partner, and then share your story with the class.

- Go to the next corner and turn left onto Center Street.
- Walk three blocks to Second Avenue and turn right.
- Walk two more blocks, and you'll see City Hall on the left.

City Hall?

A. Excuse me. **Can you tell me**[1] how to get to City Hall?

B. Yes. Go to the next corner and turn left onto Center Street. Walk three blocks to Second Avenue and turn right. Walk two more blocks, and you'll see City Hall on the left.

A. I'm sorry. **I didn't follow you.**[2] **Could you please repeat that?**[3]

B. **Okay.**[4] First, go to the next corner and turn left onto Center Street.

A. **Uh-húh.**[5]

B. Then walk three blocks to Second Avenue and turn right. **Are you with me so far?**[6]

A. Yes. **I'm following you.**[7]

B. Then walk two more blocks, and you'll see City Hall on the left. Have you got all that?

A. Yes. **Now I've got it.**[8] Thanks very much.

---

[1] Could you tell me
Do you know

[2] I didn't get that.

[3] Could you please say that again?

[4] Sure.
All right.

[5] Um-hmm.
Okay.

[6] Okay so far?
Are you following me so far?

[7] I understand.
I'm with you.

[8] Now I understand.

A. Excuse me. **Can you tell me**[1] how to get to _____?

B. Yes. _____.
_____.
_____.

A. I'm sorry. **I didn't follow you.**[2] **Could you please repeat that?**[3]

B. **Okay.**[4] First, _____.

A. **Uh-húh.**[5]

B. Then _____.
Are you with me so far?[6]

A. Yes. **I'm following you.**[7]

B. Then _____.
Have you got all that?

A. Yes. **Now I've got it.**[8] Thanks very much.

- _Take a left at the next intersection._
- _Drive about five or six blocks to Main Street and turn right._
- _Follow Main Street all the way to the end, and you'll see the Acme Furniture Company on the left._

1 the Acme Furniture Company?

- _Walk down this street to Park Avenue and turn right._
- _Walk along Park Avenue a few blocks, and you'll come to a big supermarket._
- _Take the first right after the supermarket, and you'll see the library in the middle of that block._

2 the library?

- _Drive down this road until you get to the first traffic light._
- _Turn left at the light, go about two miles, and you'll see a sign for the interstate._
- _Take the interstate north to Exit 7, and that will take you directly to the zoo._

3 the zoo?

Ask how to get someplace.

Listen

Listen and follow the directions to different places. Write the letter of the place people are talking about in each conversation.

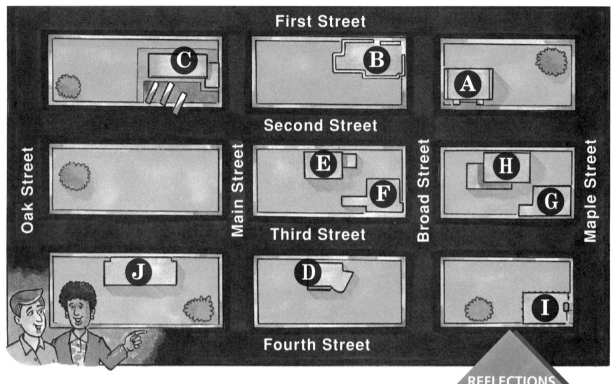

1. ___F___   4. _____   7. _____

2. _____   5. _____   8. _____

3. _____   6. _____   9. _____

REFLECTIONS
Is it easy or difficult for people to get around town where you live? Do people need cars? How is the public transportation system? Do you have any problems getting around town? How can your community solve these problems?

Discuss in pairs or small groups, and then share your ideas with the class.

Matching Lines

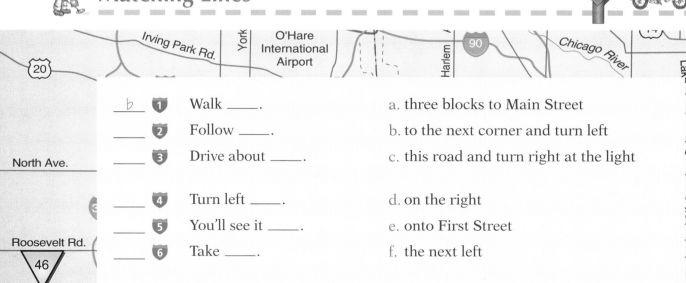

_b_ 1. Walk _____.   a. three blocks to Main Street

____ 2. Follow _____.   b. to the next corner and turn left

____ 3. Drive about _____.   c. this road and turn right at the light

____ 4. Turn left _____.   d. on the right

____ 5. You'll see it _____. e. onto First Street

____ 6. Take _____.   f. the next left

Choose the Right Way

Choose the correct answer.

1 _____ know how to get to Route 1?
a. Could you
b. Are you
c. Do you *(circled)*

2 Are you _____?
a. following you
b. with me
c. understand

3 Could you _____ again?
a. please
b. say that
c. follow

4 Now I've _____.
a. understand
b. following you
c. got it

5 Have you _____?
a. with me so far
b. got all that
c. please repeat that

6 Can you _____?
a. tell me how to get there
b. following me so far
c. know how to get there

7 Now I _____.
a. understand
b. didn't get that
c. with you

8 _____ repeat that?
a. Do you
b. Could you please
c. Have you

Listen

Listen to the conversation. Did the person understand the directions?

1 a. Yes *(circled)*
b. No

2 a. Yes
b. No

3 a. Yes
b. No

4 a. Yes
b. No

5 a. Yes
b. No

6 a. Yes
b. No

7 a. Yes
b. No

8 a. Yes
b. No

9 a. Yes
b. No

Figure It Out!

With a partner, think of a "mystery location" — a well-known place in your community. Write out a set of directions to get to this place. Then role-play a scene in which one person gives directions to the other, but doesn't name the place. Can other students guess the "mystery location"?

INTERCHANGE

I'm Lost!

A. Hello.

B. Hello, Bob? This is Larry.

A. Larry! Where ARE you?

B. I'm lost!

A. You're lost?!

B. I'm afraid so.

A. Did you follow my directions?

B. I think so. I went north on Union Boulevard to Elm Street.

A. Yes, that's right.

B. Then I turned right and drove to Washington Avenue.

A. Um-hmm.

B. After that, I took the parkway south and got off at Exit 14.

A. Uh-oh! That's the problem. You were supposed to get off at Exit 15.

B. Oh.

A. Where are you now?

B. I'm calling from a phone at the Westover Supermarket.

A. Oh, that's not far from here. Here's what you should do. Go to the corner and turn right at Station Street. Follow Station Street about seven blocks. Turn right on Blake Road, and you'll see my house at the end of the block on the left. Have you got that?

B. I think so. Let me see. I go to the corner and turn right at Station Street.

A. Uh-húh.

B. Then I follow Station Street about seven blocks.

A. Um-hmm.

B. And then . . . hmm . . . Could you repeat the last part?

A. Yes. Turn right on Blake Road, and you'll see my house at the end of the block on the left.

B. Okay. I've got it now. Thanks. I'll be there in a few minutes.

A. Hello.

B. Hello, _____? This is _____.

A. _____! Where ARE you?

B. I'm lost!

A. You're lost?!

B. I'm afraid so.

A. Did you follow my directions?

B. I think so. I _____.

A. Yes, that's right.

B. Then I _____.

A. Uh-hḿm.

B. After that, I _____.

A. Uh-oh! That's the problem. You were supposed to _____.

B. Oh.

A. Where are you now?

B. I'm calling from a phone at _____.

A. Oh, that's not far from here. Here's what you should do.

_____.

_____.

_____.

Have you got that?

B. I think so. Let me see. I _____.

A. Uh-húh.

B. Then I _____.

A. Um-hḿm.

B. And then . . . hmm . . . Could you repeat the last part?

A. Yes. _____.

B. Okay. I've got it now. Thanks. I'll be there in a few minutes.

Write out directions to the home of a friend. Write the directions in 5 steps, but make a mistake in the 3rd direction.

1. _____

2. _____

3. _____

4. _____

5. _____

You're on your way to your friend's house, and you're lost! The third direction you write down is wrong. Call your friend to say you're lost, using your set of directions and the model dialog above as a guide. Feel free to adapt and expand the model any way you wish.

Rush hour traffic is a problem in many big cities around the world. Commuters rush to and from their jobs in cars, buses, subways, trains, and even on bicycles. Large cities in the United States have two rush hours—one in the morning and one in the evening. But in cities in other parts of the world, there are four rush hours. In Athens and Rome, for example, many workers go home for lunch and a nap. After this midday break, they rush back to their jobs and work for a few more hours.

In Tokyo, there's a big rush hour underground. Most of the people in Tokyo take the subways. The trains are very crowded. Subway employees called *packers* wear white gloves and help *pack* the commuters into the trains when the doors close. They make sure that all purses, briefcases, clothes, and hands are inside the trains.

In Seoul, many commuters prefer to take taxis to get to work. To *hail a cab*, many people stand at intersections and raise two fingers. This means they'll pay the cab driver double the usual fare. Some people even raise three fingers! They'll pay THREE times the normal rate.

Streets in Rome are very crowded with automobiles and mopeds during rush hours. The city can't make its streets wider, and it can't build new highways, because it doesn't want to disturb the many historic sites in the city, such as the Forum and the Colosseum. It took the city fifteen years to construct a new subway system. Construction had to stop every time workers found old artifacts and discovered places of interest to archaeologists.

Athens is another ancient city that cannot build large highways. To deal with rush hour problems, the city government decided to cut traffic in half. Drivers with license plate numbers ending in 0 through 4 can drive only on certain days. Drivers with numbers ending in 5 through 9 can drive on the other days.

In many big cities, there are special lanes on highways for carpools. These are groups of three or more people who drive to and from work together. They share the costs of gas and parking and take turns driving into the city.

Getting to work and getting home can be difficult in many places around the world. Rush hour traffic seems to be a universal problem.

True or False?

1. All commuters have cars or bicycles.

2. Subways in Tokyo are crowded because most people don't drive. They take the train.

3. In Seoul, people have to pay double the normal taxi fare.

4. There aren't any large highways in Athens or Rome because of the historic sites in these cities.

5. In many big cities, commuters have to drive to work in carpools.

6. Rush hour is a problem only in Athens, Rome, Seoul, Washington, D.C., and other cities in the United States.

Do You Remember?

Try to answer these questions without looking back at the reading.

1. Big cities have problems during rush hour because there are ____.
   a. special lanes on highways
   b. many commuters
   c. four rush hours

2. Most of the commuters in Tokyo ____.
   a. take subway trains to work
   b. are packers
   c. take taxis

3. To *hail a cab* means to ____.
   a. pay double the normal rate
   b. try to get a cab
   c. prefer to take taxis

4. It took a long time to build a subway system in Rome because ____.
   a. the streets are very crowded
   b. there are many historic sites
   c. the workers discovered many artifacts and places of interest

5. Commuters in carpools probably ____.
   a. live in the city
   b. take the subway to work
   c. save money on gas and parking fees

6. All carpools ____.
   a. are a universal problem
   b. have more than one person
   c. have special license plates

Your Turn

For Writing and Discussion

Tell how people in your community get around town.

Do they drive, or do they take buses and trains?
Are taxis very common?
Do people ride bicycles?

Tell about traffic where you live.

When is rush hour?
Is there a lot of traffic in your community?
Do you have any advice for ways to avoid difficult traffic areas?

51

Asking for Information
How do you spell that?
Can you spell that?

Can you tell me _____?
Could you tell me _____?
Do you know _____?

Certainty
Are you sure _____?
Are you certain _____?
Are you positive _____?

I think so.
I'm pretty sure.

Apologizing
I apologize.
Excuse me.
I'm sorry.

Attracting Attention
Excuse me.
Pardon me.

Checking Someone's Understanding
Are you with me so far?
Okay so far?
Are you following me so far?

Indicating Understanding
Yes.
Uh-húh.
Um-hḿm.
That's right.
Okay.

I'm following you.
I understand.
I'm with you.

Now I've got it.
Now I understand.

Gratitude
Thank you.
Thanks.
Thank you very much.
Thanks very much.

Surprise-Disbelief
I don't believe it!
I can't believe it!

Obligation
I've got to _____.
I have to _____.
I need to _____.

Hesitating
Let me see.
Let's see.

Asking for Repetition
(I'm sorry.) I didn't follow you.
(I'm sorry.) I didn't get that.

Could you please repeat that?
Could you please say that again?

Now Leaving Exit 3 Construction Area

- ☐ **Question Formation**
- ☐ **Negative Sentences**
- ☐ **Simple Present Tense**
- ☐ **Past Tense**
- ☐ **Imperatives**
- ☐ **Have to / Have Got to**

Sorry for the inconvenience. For more information see pages 160 and 161.

ExpressWays Checklist
I can . . .

- ☐ call directory assistance
- ☐ make telephone calls
- ☐ access public transportation
- ☐ give directions to places in the community
- ☐ give someone directions by car

REST STOP
Take a break!
Have a conversation!

Here are some scenes from Exits 1, 2, and 3.

Who do you think these people are?
What do you think they're talking about?

In pairs or small groups, create conversations based on these scenes and act them out.

Exit 4

HOUSING AND FOOD

Take Exit 4 to . . .

➤ Describe features of an apartment, using singular/plural and adjectives

➤ Enumerate food items, using count/non-count nouns and partitives

➤ Locate items in a supermarket, using count/non-count nouns

➤ Evaluate the cost of food items, using count/non-count nouns

➤ Discuss ingredients, using count/non-count nouns

➤ Give recipe instructions, using imperatives

Functions This Exit!

Want-Desire
Asking for and Reporting
   Information
Directions-Location
Describing
Complimenting
Instructing
Surprise-Disbelief
Gratitude
Agreement/Disagreement
Clarification

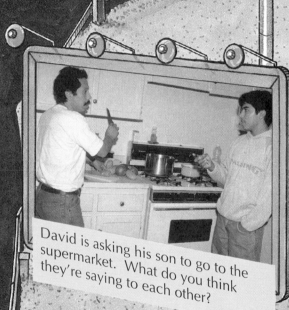

David is asking his son to go to the supermarket. What do you think they're saying to each other?

Anthony is at Sonia's house for dinner. They're talking about the food. What do you think they're saying to each other?

A. How can I help you?

B. We're looking for a two-bedroom apartment downtown.

A. Hmm. A two-bedroom apartment downtown. I think I have just what you're looking for.

B. Oh, good. Where is it?

A. It's on Dixon Street.

B. What kind of neighborhood is it?

A. I think you'll like the neighborhood. It's very safe.

B. That sounds good. What can you tell us about the apartment?

A. Well, you'll love the kitchen! It has a brand new refrigerator. And believe me, you don't find many two-bedroom apartments downtown with brand new refrigerators!

B. Hmm. Another question. Are dogs allowed in the building?

A. Dogs? Yes, I believe they are.

B. How much is the rent?

A. $800 a month.

B. Does that include utilities?

A. Everything except gas. Would you like to see the apartment?

B. Yes, I think so.

A. How can I help you?

B. (We're/I'm) looking for a _____-bedroom apartment _____.

A. Hmm. A _____-bedroom apartment _____. I think I have just what you're looking for.

B. Oh, good. Where is it?

A. It's on _____.

B. What kind of neighborhood is it?

A. I think you'll like the neighborhood. It's very _____.

B. That sounds good. What can you tell (us/me) about the apartment?

A. Well, you'll love the kitchen! It has a brand new _____. And believe me, you don't find many _____-bedroom apartments _____ with brand new _____s!

B. Hmm. Another question. Are _____s allowed in the building?

A. _____s? Yes, I believe they are.

B. How much is the rent?

A. $_____ a month.

B. Does that include utilities?

A. Everything except _____. Would you like to see the apartment?

B. Yes, I think so.

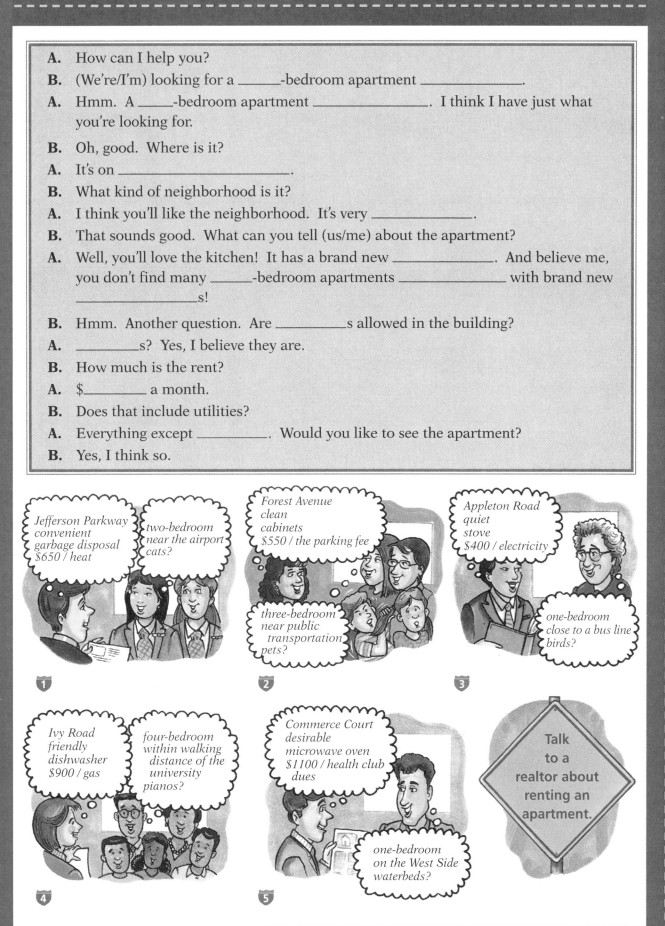

Jefferson Parkway
convenient
garbage disposal
$650 / heat

two-bedroom
near the airport
cats?

1

Forest Avenue
clean
cabinets
$550 / the parking fee

three-bedroom
near public
transportation
pets?

2

Appleton Road
quiet
stove
$400 / electricity

one-bedroom
close to a bus line
birds?

3

Ivy Road
friendly
dishwasher
$900 / gas

four-bedroom
within walking
distance of the
university
pianos?

4

Commerce Court
desirable
microwave oven
$1100 / health club
dues

one-bedroom
on the West Side
waterbeds?

5

Talk
to a
realtor about
renting an
apartment.

Fill It In!

Fill in the correct answer.

1 It's a _____ stove.
   a. convenient
   (b.) brand new

2 This is a _____ neighborhood.
   a. walking distance
   b. quiet

3 The cabinets are very _____.
   a. friendly
   b. clean

4 The rent is _____.
   a. $650
   b. safe

5 Is it a _____ neighborhood?
   a. comfortable
   b. desirable

6 The neighbors are _____.
   a. quiet
   b. like

7 The building is _____.
   a. allowed
   b. safe

8 The apartment is _____ to a bus line.
   a. near
   b. close

Apartment Match

apt.	= apartment	kit.	= kitchen
a/c	= air conditioning	lge.	= large
avail.	= available	loc.	= location
BR	= bedroom	mo.	= month
bldg.	= building	mod.	= modern
conv.	= convenient	trans.	= transportation
elec.	= electricity	utils.	= utilities
fpl.	= fireplace	W/D	= washer & dryer
incl.	= including	w/	= with

_c_ **1** 2 BR   a. The apartment has a modern kitchen.

___ **2** 2 apts. avail.   b. The apartment has air conditioning.

___ **3** 1 BR apt.   c. It's a two-bedroom apartment.

___ **4** w/mod. kit.   d. The apartment is near transportation.

___ **5** incl. utils.   e. The rent includes utilities.

___ **6** lge. BR   f. There are two apartments for rent.

___ **7** near trans.   g. The apartment has a washer and dryer.

___ **8** conv. loc.   h. The apartment has a large bedroom.

___ **9** $400 mo.   i. The rent is four hundred dollars a month.

___ **10** w/fpl.   j. It's a one-bedroom apartment.

___ **11** w/a/c   k. The apartment has a fireplace.

___ **12** w/W/D   l. The apartment is in a convenient location.

Which Apartment?

A **DOWNTOWN AREA**/123 Kent St.
2BR, a/c, fpl., conv. loc.
$650 mo. plus utils.
276-1274

B **PARK HILL**/160 Park Rd.
2 lge. 1 BR apts. avail.,
mod. kit. $595 + utils.
622-0567

C 143 Spring Rd./3BR
W/D, fpl., conv. trans.
$750 mo. + utils. 524-3920

D **OAK VALLEY**/4356 Oak Ave.
2 BR lge. kit. a/c, $550 mo.
incl. utils. 338-5607

We're looking for a three-bedroom apartment.

1 ___C___

I'd like an apartment with air conditioning and a fireplace.

2 _____

We need a washer and dryer in the apartment.

3 _____

We'd like a two-bedroom apartment, but we can't pay more than $600.

4 _____

Do you have an apartment downtown?

5 _____

I'd like an apartment with a modern kitchen.

6 _____

Is there anything available in Oak Valley?

7 _____

We're going to need two apartments.

8 _____

We'd like the utilities included in our rent.

9 _____

InterActions

The people on pages 56 and 57 are now looking at the apartments. Are the apartments as nice as the realtor said they were? In pairs or in small groups, choose one of the situations and re-enact a visit to the apartment with the realtor. Present your role play to the class, and then compare what happened during the different apartment visits.

sugar—a small bag
oranges—4
milk—a half gallon

A. Could you do me a favor?

B. **Sure.**[1] What is it?

A. Could you run over to the store? We need a few things.

B. **All right.**[2] What do you want me to get?

A. Well, could you pick up some sugar?

B. Okay. How much?

A. A small bag. I guess we also need a few oranges.

B. How many?

A. **Let's see**[3] . . . How about four?

B. Anything else?

A. Yes. We're out of milk.

B. Okay. How much do you want me to get?

A. I think a half gallon will be enough.

B. Is that everything?

A. I think so.

B. Okay. So that's a small bag of sugar, four oranges, and a half gallon of milk.

A. That's right. **Thanks.**[4] I really appreciate it.

B. My pleasure.

[1] Certainly.   [2] Okay.   [3] Let me see . . .   [4] Thanks very much.
         Sure.   Let me think . . .   Thank you.
                                            Thank you very much.
                                            Thanks a lot.

A. Could you do me a favor?
B. **Sure.**[1] What is it?
A. Could you run over to the store? We need a few things.
B. **All right.**[2] What do you want me to get?
A. Well, could you pick up some _____?
B. Okay. How much?
A. _____. I guess we also need a few _____s.
B. How many?
A. **Let's see**[3] . . . How about _____?
B. Anything else?
A. Yes. We're out of _____.
B. Okay. How much do you want me to get?
A. I think _____ will be enough.
B. Is that everything?
A. I think so.
B. Okay. So that's _____, _____, and _____.
A. That's right. **Thanks.**[4] I really appreciate it.
B. My pleasure.

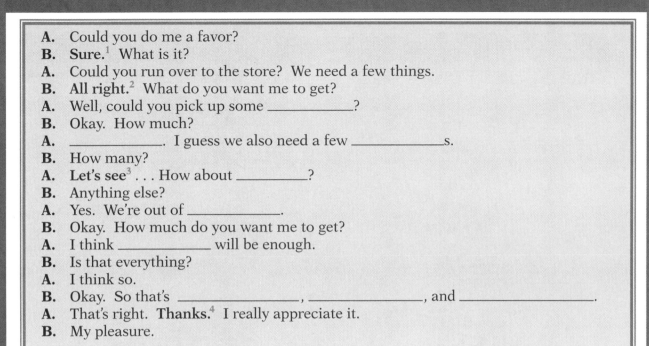

1.
peanut butter — a big jar
potatoes — 3
orange juice — 1 quart

2.
coffee — a pound
eggs — half a dozen
chocolate ice cream — a pint

3.
white bread — 1 loaf
bananas — a small bunch
Swiss cheese — half a pound

4.
rice — a medium-size box
onions — 5 or 6
ground beef — a pound and
a half

5.
mayonnaise — an 8-ounce jar
lemons — 3 or 4
tuna fish — 1 can

6.
orange soda — a six-pack
apples — 7 or 8
butter — 2 sticks

7.
lettuce — 2 heads
green peppers — 3
toothpaste — the regular-size
tube

8.
yogurt — 3 small containers
avocados — 2
mineral water — 2 bottles

**Ask a favor.
You need a few
things at the
supermarket.**

61

Shopping Lists

| can | bag | gallon | box |
| tube | liter | pound | jar |

Don't forget . . .

a can of	tuna fish
two bags of	potato chips
	crackers
	cheese
	mineral water

1. The Baxters are going to have a party tonight. Complete their shopping list.

| bunch | six-pack | loaf | stick |
| dozen | pint | jar | pound |

Don't forget . . .

	bread
	grapes
	soda
	mayonnaise
	butter

2. A few of Peter's friends are coming to visit tomorrow afternoon. Complete Peter's shopping list.

| tube | jar | box | container |
| loaf | head | bag | gallon |

Don't forget . . .

	milk
	peanut butter
	white bread
	toothpaste
	cookies

3. Mrs. King's grandchildren are planning to visit her for the weekend. Complete her shopping list.

| gallon | container | bottle | bag |
| pound | dozen | can | liter |

Don't forget . . .

	eggs
	sugar
	vanilla ice cream
	margarine
	yogurt

4. It's Tommy's birthday. His mother is going to make his favorite cake. Complete her shopping list.

The Right Choice

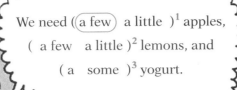

We need ((a few) a little)[1] apples, (a few a little)[2] lemons, and (a some)[3] yogurt.

Okay. Do you want me to get (a some)[4] milk, too?

How (many much)[5] sugar do you want me to get?

A large bag. I guess we also need (a some)[6] mayonnaise.

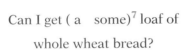

Can I get (a some)[7] loaf of whole wheat bread?

Sure. And how about (a some)[8] cheese and (a few a little)[9] avocados, too?

Could you pick up (a few a little)[10] bananas at the supermarket?

Okay. And we also need (a some)[11] butter and (a few a little)[12] potatoes.

Listen

Listen and complete the sentence.

1. a. (eggs)
   b. coffee

2. a. tuna fish
   b. ice cream

3. a. orange juice
   b. peanut butter

4. a. lemons
   b. toothpaste

5. a. ground beef
   b. rice

6. a. lettuce
   b. cheese

7. a. butter
   b. onion

8. a. tomatoes
   b. sugar

CrossTalk

Work in small groups and plan a class party. Decide what food you'd like to serve and how much you need to buy. Then discuss each group's menu as a class and vote to choose one. If your teacher agrees, buy the food and have a party!

63

A. **Excuse me.**[1] Where can I find yogurt?

B. Yogurt? It's in the Dairy Section, Aisle B.

A. I'm sorry. **Did you say**[2] Aisle D?

B. No, "B."

A. Oh. Thanks very much.

B. You're welcome.[3]

[1] Pardon me.

[2] Was that

[3] My pleasure.
Any time.

1

2

3

4

5

You're looking for something at the supermarket.

Match and Practice

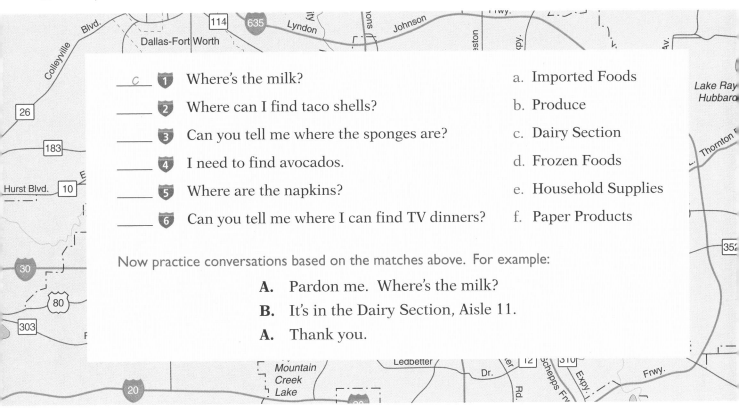

_c_ **1** Where's the milk?

_____ **2** Where can I find taco shells?

_____ **3** Can you tell me where the sponges are?

_____ **4** I need to find avocados.

_____ **5** Where are the napkins?

_____ **6** Can you tell me where I can find TV dinners?

a. Imported Foods

b. Produce

c. Dairy Section

d. Frozen Foods

e. Household Supplies

f. Paper Products

Now practice conversations based on the matches above. For example:

A. Pardon me. Where's the milk?

B. It's in the Dairy Section, Aisle 11.

A. Thank you.

Listen

Listen and choose the letter or number you hear.

1
a. 3
b. C

2
a. 8
b. H

3
a. A
b. J

4
a. 8
b. A

5
a. C
b. D

6
a. G
b. J

7
a. 4
b. 14

8
a. M
b. N

9
a. 70
b. 17

10
a. S
b. F

Community Connections

Visit a local supermarket and find out the following information:

How many aisles are there in the supermarket?
What are the names of the different sections?
Does the store offer services such as check cashing and film developing?
What other services does the supermarket offer?
What are the different kinds of jobs you see people doing?

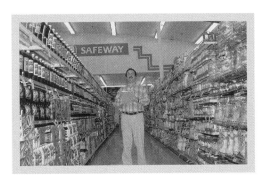

Also, interview a person who works there and ask about that person's job responsibilities. Report your findings to the class and compare different supermarkets in your area.

65

It's Amazing How Little You Can Buy!

A. Okay. That comes to twelve dollars and forty-nine cents.

B. Twelve dollars and forty-nine cents?! Are you sure that's right? That seems a little high to me.

A. Well, let's see. The vitamins were six ninety-four. The skim milk was a dollar seventeen. The bean sprouts were ninety-nine cents. And the diet soda was three thirty-nine. That comes to a total of twelve dollars and forty-nine cents.

B. Hmm. **How about that!**[1] It's amazing how little you can buy these days for twelve dollars and forty-nine cents!

A. You're right.[2]

---

[1] How do you like that!
Isn't that something!

[2] That's true.
[*less formal*]
I'll say!
You can say THAT again!

```
vitamins -
          $6.94
skim milk -
          $1.17
bean
sprouts -
           $.99
diet soda -
          $3.39
_____
          $12.49
```

```
hot dogs -
          $6.00
baked beans -
          $1.89
mustard -
           $.98
apple pie -
          $4.50
_____
          $13.37
```

1

```
pretzels -
          $1.58
potato
chips -
           $.99
popcorn -
          $1.38
soda -
          $7.98
_____
          $11.93
```

2

```
spaghetti -
          $2.65
potatoes -
          $1.98
ice cream -
          $4.79
chocolate
chip cookies -
          $1.89
_____
          $11.31
```

3

```
artichokes -
          $2.40
garlic -
           1.80
mushrooms -
          $5.00
coffee -
          $7.89
_____
          $17.09
```

4

```
tea -
          $2.79
crackers -
          $1.69
prunes -
          $2.19
cat food -
          $8.40
_____
          $15.07
```

5

> You can't believe how much things cost at the supermarket! Talk to the cashier.

Listen

What prices do you hear?

1. a. $14.50
   b. $13.15

2. a. $ 8.10
   b. $18.10

3. a. $11.40
   b. $ 7.40

4. a. $16.43
   b. $ 6.43

5. a. $14.66
   b. $15.76

6. a. $30.58
   b. $13.58

7. a. $22.11
   b. $33.87

8. a. $18.98
   b. $19.88

9. a. $ 9.98
   b. $19.89

CrossTalk

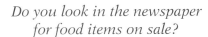

Do you look in the newspaper for food items on sale?

Do you cut out coupons?

Do you compare prices at different stores?

What are different ways you can save money on food? Brainstorm with a partner and then share as a class. Make a master list of everybody's suggestions.

Comparison Shopping

How well do you know the cost of food these days?

With a group of students, make up a shopping list of ten supermarket items. On a separate piece of paper, write down what you think each item costs. Give your list to another group, and those students will write down what THEY think the items cost.

Then go to different supermarkets and find out the actual prices of the items. Report back to the class and compare the prices at different stores. Which group guessed the prices most correctly?

Discuss the prices as a class. Were some of the items cheaper than you thought? Were other items more expensive than you thought?

A. Mmm! These are **delicious!**[1] What are they?

B. They're enchiladas.

A. Enchiladas?

B. Yes. They're a popular Mexican dish.

A. Well, they're **excellent.**[1] What's in them?

B. **Let's see**[2]. . . a little flour, a little cheese, a few tomatoes, and . . . uh, oh yes, a little ground beef.

A. Are they difficult to make?

B. No, not at all. I'll be happy to give you the recipe.

A. Thanks.

[1] excellent
wonderful
superb
fantastic

[2] Let me see . . .
Let me think . . .

These are delicious!

*flour
cheese
tomatoes
ground beef*

enchiladas
Mexican

This is excellent!

*water
beets
sour cream
onions*

1 borscht
Russian

These are wonderful!

*flour
water
eggs
milk*

2 waffles
American

This is superb!

*eggplants
ground beef
tomato sauce
mushrooms*

3 moussaka
Greek

This is delicous!

*eggs
flour
Italian cheese
tomato sauce*

4 manicotti
Italian

These are fantastic!

*pork
cabbage
bean sprouts
M.S.G. ***

5 egg rolls
Chinese

Compliment a friend on his or her food.

* M.S.G. = Monosodium Glutamate

ExpressWays

it	a few
them	a little

Mmm! This apple pie is delicious! What's in ___it___¹?

_____² apples, of course, _____³ sugar, _____⁴ flour, _____⁵ raisins, _____⁶ butter, and _____⁷ lemon juice.

These rolls are wonderful! What do you put in _____⁸?

I use _____⁹ margarine, _____¹⁰ flour, _____¹¹ eggs, _____¹² milk, _____¹³ poppy seeds, and _____¹⁴ cinammon.

Listen

Listen and decide what the people are talking about.

1. a. egg rolls
   b. lettuce

2. a. tomato
   b. utility bill

3. a. pork
   b. mall

4. a. house
   b. refrigerator

5. a. recipe
   b. lemon

6. a. apartment
   b. dog

CrossTalk

Talk with a partner about your favorite food.

What is it?
Why do you like it?
What are the ingredients?
Is it easy or difficult to make?
Who prepares it the best? you? your wife or husband? your mother or father? a favorite restaurant?

Could I Ask You for the Recipe?

A. Your meat loaf was delicious!

B. Oh, did you really like it?

A. Yes. Very much. It was excellent!

B. Thank you for saying so.

A. Could I ask you for the recipe?

B. Sure. It's really very easy. First, mix together one egg, two teaspoons of salt, and two pounds of ground beef. Then add half a cup of milk and a cup of bread crumbs. Are you with me so far?

A. Yes, I'm with you.

B. Okay. Next, put the mixture into a greased baking pan. And after that, bake for an hour and fifteen minutes at 350 degrees.

A. Wait a minute! I didn't get the last step. Could you repeat that part?

B. Sure. Bake for an hour and fifteen minutes at 350 degrees.

A. Now I've got it. Is that it?

B. Yes. That's it!

A. Thanks very much.

B. My pleasure.

A. Your _____ (was/were) delicious!

B. Oh, did you really like (it/them)?

A. Yes. Very much. (It was/They were) excellent!

B. Thank you for saying so.

A. Could I ask you for the recipe?

B. Sure. It's really very easy. First, _____.
Then _____.
Are you with me so far?

A. Yes, I'm with you.

B. Okay. Next, _____.
And after that, _____.

A. Wait a minute! I didn't get the last step. Could you repeat that part?

B. Sure. _____.

A. Now I've got it. Is that it?

B. Yes. That's it!

A. Thanks very much.

B. My pleasure.

You're a dinner guest at somebody's home. You enjoyed the food very much. One dish was especially good. Compliment the host or hostess and ask for the recipe, using the model dialog above as a guide. Feel free to adapt and expand the model any way you wish.

Your Turn

For Writing and Discussion

Now share YOUR favorite recipe.

_____
_____
_____
_____
_____
_____
_____
_____
_____
_____

REFLECTIONS
Do you have healthy eating habits? What kinds of food do you like? In your opinion, what foods are good for people? What foods are bad for people? How can you improve your diet?

Discuss in pairs or small groups, and then share your ideas with the class.

Some supermarkets are enormous these days, with aisles and aisles of different kinds of foods and products. For example, you can find fifteen to twenty different kinds of cheese in the Dairy section. You can find many different brands of toilet tissue in the Paper Products section. The Frozen Food section has everything from cans of frozen apple juice to bags of mixed vegetables and frozen pizza.

Many supermarkets also have a big Health Care Products aisle. This section is like a small drug store, with different brands of medicines, shampoos, toothpastes, and other health care items. Some supermarkets even sell magazines, books, shoes, underwear, hammers, screwdrivers, and other household products.

Many supermarkets offer services, too. You can leave your film there and return the next day to get your photographs. You can use a special card in *money machines* to take money out of your bank. In some supermarkets, you can even rent floor polishers, carpet cleaners, and movies!

Shoppers in many supermarkets can buy snacks and cold drinks from vending machines. In some places, tired, hungry shoppers can sit down and enjoy a fresh cup of coffee and a donut at a supermarket snack bar or coffee shop.

These huge supermarkets with their large variety of goods and services are not the only places to buy food. There are also smaller grocery stores. These stores usually carry the same food products as the large supermarkets, but they don't usually have as wide a selection. Grocery stores are often in locations convenient for people who don't drive. Some cities

also have specialty stores such as fish markets, butcher shops, and bakeries. Years ago, these little shops were very common, but in many places they are less common today. Supermarkets, with their variety of products and services, are much more popular.

True or False?

1. There are many different kinds of food markets in the United States.
2. People can go to supermarkets to buy household products.
3. According to the reading, most shoppers today go to specialty stores.
4. Shoppers can eat and drink at some supermarkets.
5. Neighborhood grocery stores are usually enormous.

Do You Remember?

Try to answer these questions without looking back at the reading.

1. Look in the Dairy section if you want to buy ____.
   a. a variety of frozen juices
   b. many kinds of milk products
   c. a wide selection of vegetables

2. The Health Care Products aisle in a supermarket has ____.
   a. items you can find in drug stores
   b. medicines only
   c. everything you can find in drug stores

3. At many supermarkets, you can ____.
   a. watch movies
   b. take money out of your bank account
   c. find smaller grocery stores

4. At a butcher shop, you can probably buy ____.
   a. butchers
   b. hammers and screwdrivers
   c. different kinds of meat

5. Many supermarkets have vending machines for people who ____.
   a. are tired
   b. are hungry or thirsty
   c. want to sit down

6. Neighborhood grocery stores carry many items, but ____.
   a. not many different types
   b. aren't in convenient locations
   c. are only for people who don't have cars

7. Fish markets, butcher shops, and bakeries are ____.
   a. in cities
   b. specialty stores
   c. for people who don't drive

8. Supermarkets are ____.
   a. specialty shops
   b. more and more expensive
   c. more common than grocery stores

Cultural Intersections

Tell about food shopping in your country.

Do people shop in supermarkets or in specialty stores?
What kinds of specialty stores are there?
How do food stores in your country compare with those in the United States?

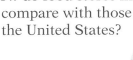

73

☐ **Gratitude**
Thanks.
Thanks very much.
Thank you.
Thank you very much.
Thanks a lot.

☐ **Responding to Gratitude**
You're welcome.
My pleasure.
Any time.

☐ **Hesitating**
Let's see . . .
Let me see . . .
Let me think . . .

☐ **Responding to Requests**
Sure.
Certainly.
All right.
Okay.

☐ **Attracting Attention**
Excuse me.
Pardon me.

☐ **Asking for Clarification**
Did you say _____?
Was that _____?

☐ **Surprise-Disbelief**
How about that!
How do you like that!
Isn't that something!

☐ **Agreement**
You're right.
That's true.
[less formal]
I'll say!
You can say THAT again!

☐ **Describing**
delicious
excellent
wonderful
superb
fantastic

Now Leaving Exit 4 Construction Area

☐ **Adjectives**
☐ **Singular / Plural**
☐ **Count / Non-Count Nouns**
☐ **Partitives**
☐ **Pronouns**
☐ **Imperatives**

Sorry for the inconvenience. For more information see pages 162 and 163.

ExpressWays Checklist

I can . . .

☐ Describe features of an apartment
☐ Enumerate food items
☐ Locate items in a supermarket
☐ Evaluate the cost of food items
☐ Discuss ingredients
☐ Give recipe instructions

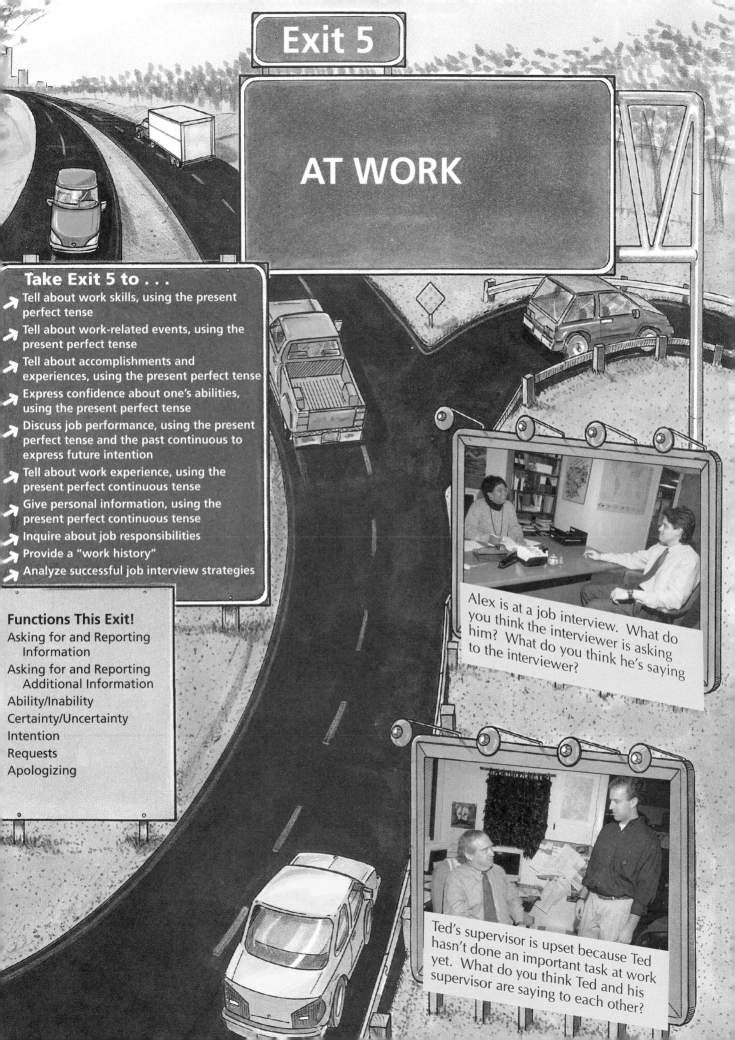

Exit 5

AT WORK

Take Exit 5 to . . .
- Tell about work skills, using the present perfect tense
- Tell about work-related events, using the present perfect tense
- Tell about accomplishments and experiences, using the present perfect tense
- Express confidence about one's abilities, using the present perfect tense
- Discuss job performance, using the present perfect tense and the past continuous to express future intention
- Tell about work experience, using the present perfect continuous tense
- Give personal information, using the present perfect continuous tense
- Inquire about job responsibilities
- Provide a "work history"
- Analyze successful job interview strategies

Functions This Exit!
Asking for and Reporting Information
Asking for and Reporting Additional Information
Ability/Inability
Certainty/Uncertainty
Intention
Requests
Apologizing

Alex is at a job interview. What do you think the interviewer is asking him? What do you think he's saying to the interviewer?

Ted's supervisor is upset because Ted hasn't done an important task at work yet. What do you think Ted and his supervisor are saying to each other?

A. I saw your sign in the window. What position do you have open?

B. We're looking for a reporter.

A. I'd like to apply.

B. Have you written obituaries before?

A. Yes, I have. I've written obituaries in my last two jobs.

B. Okay. Here's an application form. You can sit over there and fill it out.

A. Thank you.

a reporter
write* obituaries

1 a stock clerk
take* inventory

2 a delivery person
drive* a van

3 a dance instructor
give* tango lessons

4 a mechanic's assistant
do* engine tune-ups

5 an assistant chef
make* sandwiches and omelettes

Ask about
a job
opening.

* write-wrote-written   drive-drove-driven   do-did-done
take-took-taken   give-gave-given   make-made-made

ExpressWays

Use the correct forms of the verbs to complete the sentences.

do ○ **drive** **give** **make** **take** ○ **write**

I ___drive___ a van in my present job, and I ___drove___ a van in my last job.

Yes. I certainly know how to ___drive___ a van!

___I've driven___ a van in my last two jobs.

I _____ tune-ups in my present job, and I _____ tune-ups in my last job.

Yes. I certainly know how to _____ tune-ups!

_____ tune-ups in my last two jobs.

1

2

I _____ advertisements in my present job, and I _____ advertisements in my last job.

Yes. I certainly know how to _____ advertisements!

_____ advertisements in my last two jobs.

I _____ inventory in my present job, and I _____ inventory in my last job.

Yes. I certainly know how to _____ inventory!

_____ inventory in my last two jobs.

3

4

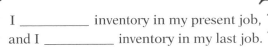

I _____ salads in my present job, and I _____ salads in my last job.

Yes. I certainly know how to _____ salads!

_____ salads in my last two jobs.

I _____ lambada lessons in my present job, and I _____ lambada lessons in my last job.

Yes. I certainly know how to _____ lambada lessons!

_____ lambada lessons in my last two jobs.

5

6

Bob
go* to the bank
this morning

A. Has Bob gone to the bank yet?
B. Yes, he has. He's already gone there.
A. Oh, good. When?
B. He went there this morning.

Barbara
speak* to her supervisor
this afternoon

A. Has Barbara spoken to her supervisor yet?
B. Yes, she has. She's already spoken to her.
A. Oh, good. When?
B. She spoke to her this afternoon.

you
see* the *top secret* report
a few minutes ago

A. Have you seen the *top secret* report yet?
B. Yes, we have. We've already seen it.
A. Oh, good. When?
B. We saw it a few minutes ago.

the employees
wear* their new uniforms
today

A. Have the employees worn their new uniforms yet?
B. Yes, they have. They've already worn them.
A. Oh, good. When?
B. They wore them today.

* go-went-gone   see-saw-seen
  speak-spoke-spoken wear-wore-worn

1 Bruno
do the dishes
a little while ago

2 Sarah
give the presentation
yesterday afternoon

3 the stock clerks
take inventory
last week

4 you
drive the new delivery van
today

5 you
meet* the new supervisor
this morning

6 Lana
read* her new contract
last night

7 Bill and Steve
get* their promotions
yesterday

8 the bank manager
go to the vault
a little while ago

9 Alberto
sing* the finale
a few minutes ago

10 you
get your Christmas bonuses
the other day

11 you
eat* in the new cafeteria
at lunchtime

12 Mr. Withers
write his letter of
resignation
an hour ago

* meet-met-met   get-got-gotten   eat-ate-eaten
read-read-read   sing-sang-sung

Constructions Ahead!

(I have)	I've	
(We have)	We've	
(You have)	You've	
(They have)	They've	} eaten.
(He has)	He's	
(She has)	She's	
(It has)	It's	

Have { I / we / you / they } eaten? Yes, { I / we / you / they } have.

Has { he / she / it } { he / she / it } has.

Construction Note: In the present perfect tense the word after *have* or *has* is a past participle. Some past participles (**met, read**) are the same as the past tense. Other past participles (**written, taken, gone**) are different from the past tense. We will tell you when the past participles are different. A list of these words is in the Appendix at the end of the book.

1 Have you ____ the memo yet?
   a. wrote
   (b.) written

2 We've already ____ the dishes.
   a. did
   b. done

3 She's already ____ to him about that.
   a. spoke
   b. spoken

4 They ____ inventory last week.
   a. took
   b. taken

5 Has she ____ the presentation yet?
   a. gave
   b. given

6 He ____ to the meeting an hour ago.
   a. went
   b. gone

8 They ____ that duet magnificently!
   a. sang
   b. sung

9 He's ____ his new tie every day this week.
   a. wore
   b. worn

10 They've already ____ that movie.
   a. saw
   b. seen

11 I've ____ at the Starlight Café many times.
   a. ate
   b. eaten

12 You've already ____ your report?!
   a. wrote
   b. written

13 I know it's ____ a long time, but I'm almost finished.
   a. took
   b. taken

7 I've ____ a truck for many years.
   a. drove
   b. driven

14 I ____ a big promotion last week!
   a. got
   b. gotten

CrossTalk

	for	**since**
I've known	many years.	1994.
	five years.	last year.
	the past few years.	I retired.
	[period of time]	*[point in time]*

I've known* how to play the piano for many years.

I've been* interested in needlepoint since I retired.

I've known how to use a computer for more than five years.

I've written several poems since I graduated from college.

I've gotten a promotion every year for the past ten years.

I've been a counselor at our local Teen Crisis Center since last July.

Talk with a partner about skills or personal experiences you're especially proud of. Then share your accomplishments with the class.

Your Turn

For Writing and Discussion

Tell about some "adventurous" things you've done in your life.

Where have you traveled?
What interesting places have you seen?
What sights have you visited?
What unusual foods have you eaten?
What interesting or unusual people have you met?

Share your adventures with others in the class.

* know-knew-known
  be-was/were-been

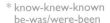

A. Have you ever flown* a 747?

B. No, I haven't, but I've flown a DC-10, and I'm confident **I'd be able to**¹ learn to fly a 747 very easily.

A. **Are you sure about that?²**

B. Oh, yes. **I'm positive.³**

¹ I could

² Are you positive about that?
Are you certain about that?
Do you really think so?

³ I'm sure.
I'm certain.
I'm a hundred percent sure.

fly a 747?

a DC-10

give ballet lessons?

tap dance lessons

1

sell computers?*

stereo equipment

2

make Italian pastries?

French pastries

3

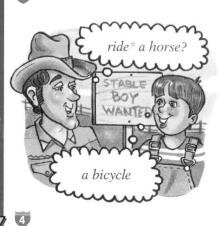

ride a horse?*

a bicycle

4

sing in a nightclub?

in my church choir

5

Express confidence at a job interview!

* fly-flew-flown
sell-sold-sold
ride-rode-ridden

Constructions Ahead!

Have	I we you they	eaten?	Yes,	I we you they	have.	No,	I we you they	haven't.
Has	he she it			he she it	has.		he she it	hasn't.

1 Have you ever (drive) ___driven___ a tractor? — No, __I haven't__.

2 Has Alan (write) _____ to the Acme Company yet? — No, _____.

3 Have the employees (go) _____ on strike yet? — Yes, _____.

4 Has Diane (do) _____ that engine tune-up yet? — Yes, _____.

5 Have you already (speak) _____ to the boss? — Yes, _____.

6 Have you and your wife ever (be) _____ to Spain? — No, _____.

7 Has this plane ever (fly) _____ to Alaska? — No, _____.

8 Have I (ask) _____ you too many questions? — Yes, _____.

Interview

Have you ever been to . . . ?

Have you ever seen . . . ?

Have you ever eaten . . . ?

Have you ever wanted to . . . ?

Think of ten "Have you ever . . . ?" questions. Interview students in your class and other people you know. What are their answers? Tell the class about unusual experiences people have had.

83

A. Have you given out the paychecks yet?

B. No, I haven't. **I was planning to**[1] give them out this afternoon.

A. **Please**[2] do it as soon as possible. The paychecks are supposed to be given out before lunch hour.

B. I'm sorry. **I didn't know that.**[3] I'll do it right away.

---

[1] I was going to

[2] Please ____.
Can you please ____?
Will you please ____?
Would you please ____?
I'd like you to ____.

[3] I didn't realize that.
I wasn't aware of that.

give out the paychecks?

this afternoon

before lunch hour

set* the tables?

in a little while

1 an hour before we open

write your monthly report?

at the end of the week

2 by the last day of the month

oil the conveyor belt?

a little later

3 at the start of every shift

polish the tables in the lobby?

after my break

4 first thing in the morning

feed* Bonzo?

pretty soon

5 at 10 o'clock sharp

You haven't done a task at work. Apologize to your supervisor.

* set-set-set
feed-fed-fed

Listen

Listen and put a check (✔) next to the task that each employee has already done and an **X** next to the task that the employee hasn't done yet.

✔ type the letters

X make copies

____ get the mail

____ speak to Mr. Chen

 1

____ fix the copy machine

____ clean the supply room

____ go to the post office

____ fill out my time sheet

 2

____ set the tables

____ put the glasses out

____ arrange the flowers

____ vacuum the floor

 3

____ write the report

____ give out the paychecks

____ eat lunch

____ meet with Mr. Cooper

 4

____ feed the animals

____ clean the cages

____ repair the van

____ walk the dog

 5

____ make the beds

____ polish the tables

____ wash the uniforms

____ read the new rules and regulations

 6

CrossTalk

Talk with a partner about work experiences you've had.

Have you ever had a supervisor or boss who was very *demanding?*
Do you think this person was fair, or did this person expect too much of you?
Tell about your experience working for this person.

A. Do you know how to¹ use a word processor?

B. Yes. I've been using word processors for a long time.

A. How long?

B. Well, let me see . . . I've been using word processors since 1990.

A. Since 1990?

B. Yes, that's right.

A. Well, you certainly have a lot of experience.

B. I guess I do.

¹ Can you
  Are you able to

use a word processor?

since 1990

operate a forklift?

since 1985

1

repair a gas heater?

for ten years

2

prepare pancakes and omelettes?

since my days as a cook in the army

3

use the Internet?

for the past five years

4

play Broadway show tunes?

since I was a teenager

5

You're at a job interview. Tell about your work experience.

Constructions Ahead!

(I have)	I've
(We have)	We've
(You have)	You've
(They have)	They've
(He has)	He's
(She has)	She's
(It has)	It's

been living here since 1990.

 1 Do you know how to type?

Yes. _I've been typing_ for a long time.

 2 Is Carmen taking inventory now?

Yes. _____ inventory since early this morning.

 3 Do they do tune-ups at Al's Garage?

Yes. _____ tune-ups there since 1992.

 4 Can Ralph sell office furniture?

Yes. _____ office furniture for the past several years.

 5 Is it still snowing?

Yes. _____ since midnight.

 6 Can you and your sister sing and dance?

Yes. _____ since we were young children.

CrossTalk

I work at Bob's Bakery. I've been working there since last July.

I live in San Francisco. I've been living there since I moved to the United states.

I study English at the Adult Language Center. I've been studying there for two years.

I take guitar lessons. I've been taking guitar lessons for the past three months. I'm not a bad guitar player!

I sing in my church choir. I've been singing in the choir since last fall. People say I have a very nice voice!

Talk with a partner. Tell some things about yourself. Ask each other questions and take notes on what your partner says. Then report to the class about your conversation.

INTERCHANGE

Can You Tell Me a Little More About the Position?

A. Can you tell me a little more[1] about the position?

B. Certainly. What would you like to know?

A. What exactly are the bookkeeper's responsibilities?

B. Well, the bookkeeper's primary responsibility is to oversee the company's finances.

A. I see.

B. In addition, the bookkeeper does the payroll. Do you think **you'd be able to**[2] handle those responsibilities?

A. Absolutely![3] In my present job, I've been overseeing the company's finances for years. And while I haven't done the payroll in my current position, I did the payroll in the job I had before that.

---

[1] Can you tell me anything more Can you tell me anything else	[2] you could	[3] Definitely! Positively!

A. Can you tell me a little more[1] about the position?

B. Certainly. What would you like to know?

A. What exactly are the _____'s responsibilities?

B. Well, the _____'s primary responsibility is to _____.

A. I see.

B. In addition, the _____ _____.
Do you think **you'd be able to**[2] handle those responsibilities?

A. Absolutely![3] In my present job, I've been _____ing for years. And while I haven't _____ in my current position, I _____ in the job I had before that.

You're at a job interview. Create an original conversation, using the model dialog above as a guide. Feel free to adapt and expand the model any way you wish.

Fill It In!

Fill in the correct answer.

1 In my present job, ____ international meetings.
   a. I've been planning
   b. I planned

2 ____ the payroll in my last position.
   a. I've done
   b. I did

3 ____ a bookkeeper at the Century Insurance Company for a long time.
   a. I'm
   b. I've been

4 In my current job, ____ new employees.
   a. I've been supervising
   b. I supervised

5 ____ all the office supplies in the job I had before.
   a. I've ordered
   b. I ordered

6 ____ three promotions since last year.
   a. I had
   b. I've had

7 ____ many different kinds of presentations in my current position.
   a. I've given
   b. I gave

8 In my last job, ____ Director of Personnel.
   a. I was
   b. I've been

Listen

Listen and choose the correct answer.

1 a. Roger takes lessons now.
   b. Roger doesn't take lessons now.

2 a. She's a student.
   b. She doesn't study Spanish now.

3 a. He's an architect.
   b. He worked as an architect.

4 a. They can ski.
   b. They didn't know how to ski when they were young.

5 a. Elena is in college.
   b. Elena is a computer programmer.

6 a. I work in Accounting.
   b. I worked in Accounting.

7 a. Irene is a receptionist.
   b. Irene has been a receptionist.

8 a. I'm unhappy at work.
   b. I was unhappy at work.

Interview

Interview a student in your class. Ask about that person's "work history."

Where have you worked?
When did you work there?
What were your responsibilities?

Do you work now?
Where do you work?
How long have you been working there?
What are your job responsibilites?

Take notes and report to the class about the person you interviewed.

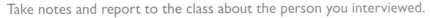

Reading: *The Job Interview*

When a job opening is advertised, there are often a lot of people interested in applying. Many job hunters send in their resumes and apply for the same position. Sometimes a company will receive hundreds of resumes for a single job opening. The job interview, therefore, is very important. In the interview, an applicant must demonstrate that he or she is the best person for the job.

Because job interviews are so critical, some job hunters read books or take courses to help them make a good first impression. These books and courses are full of advice and suggestions to help job applicants prepare for their interviews. For example, successful applicants dress appropriately and have a clean and neat appearance. They take their resume, a listing of their education and work experience, with them to the interview. They also prepare a list of questions about the job or the company. They go to the interview alone and are always on time.

At the beginning of the interview, the applicant shakes hands firmly with the employer. The employer usually invites the applicant to sit down. During the interview, it is appropriate to smile often and to look directly into the eyes of the interviewer. The applicant doesn't chew gum or smoke during the interview. The applicant is prepared to answer questions about education and previous jobs. More difficult questions are possible, such as "Why did you leave your last position?" Sometimes interviewers also try to get to know the applicant better. They ask questions about the applicant's personal background, family, and hobbies. Interviewers expect applicants to talk proudly, confidently, and truthfully about their work experience, skills, goals, and abilities. When the interview is over, the applicant stands up, shakes hands with the interviewer, and says thank you for the time the person has spent.

Job applicants who can show they are capable, well-prepared, punctual, polite, and honest have a better chance of getting the job they're looking for.

True or False?

1. Job hunters often have interviews with employers before they apply.
2. It is important to perform well during job interviews.
3. Job applicants really shouldn't ask questions during an interview.
4. Employers sometimes ask questions about the applicant's family and personal life.
5. Most employers think experience is the most important quality to have.

What's the Answer?

1 The job interview is important because ____.
   a. all the applicants for a single position have to have interviews
   b. the applicant must show that he or she is capable
   c. the applicant must be on time

2 When an applicant smiles during an interview, it is considered ____.
   a. polite and friendly
   b. funny
   c. a mistake

3 Job hunters read books and take courses ____.
   a. after they have successful job interviews
   b. if they are well-prepared
   c. to prepare themselves for their job interviews

4 It is important to be punctual for a job interview because ____.
   a. even women shake hands
   b. it is considered impolite to be late
   c. job applicants should always be neat and clean

5 It is a good idea to talk about your skills and abilities during the interview, but it isn't a good idea to ____.
   a. talk proudly
   b. look directly into the eyes of the interviewer
   c. lie

Figure It Out!

With a partner, make a list of "DOs and DON'Ts" — ten things you think a job applicant should do before and during a job interview, and ten things a job applicant shouldn't do.

Read your list to the class. For each item, have students decide: Is this something a job applicant should do or shouldn't do? After you have finished, make a master list of the most important "DOs and DON'Ts" for job interviews.

InterActions

With a partner, create a role play of a job interview. Use either the list of "DOs" or the list of "DON'Ts" to create your situation. Present your role play and let the class decide: Was the interview successful or unsuccessful?

Looking Back

Asking about Ability

Do you know how to _____?
Can you _____?
Are you able to _____?

Do you think you'd be able to _____?
Do you think you could _____?

Expressing Ability

I'm confident I'd be able to _____.
I'm confident I could _____.

Asking about Certainty

Are you sure about that?
Are you positive about that?
Are you certain about that?
Do you really think so?

Expressing Certainty

I'm positive.
I'm sure.
I'm certain.
I'm a hundred percent sure.

Absolutely!
Definitely!
Positively!

Intention

I was planning to _____.
I was going to _____.

Requests

Please _____.
Can you please _____?
Will you please _____?
Would you please _____?
I'd like you to _____.

Asking for and Reporting Additional Information

Can you tell me a little more?
Can you tell me anything more?
Can you tell me anything else?

Apologizing

I'm sorry. I didn't know that.
I'm sorry. I didn't realize that.
I'm sorry. I wasn't aware of that.

Now Leaving Exit 5 Construction Area

- [ ] **Present Perfect Tense**
- [ ] **Since/For**
- [ ] **Present Perfect Continuous Tense**
- [ ] **Contrast: Present Perfect, Present Perfect Continuous, and Past Tenses**
- [ ] **Past Continuous to Express Future Intention**

Sorry for the inconvenience. For more information see pages 164 and 165.

ExpressWays Checklist

I can . . .

- [ ] tell about my work skills
- [ ] tell about work-related events
- [ ] tell about accomplishments and experiences
- [ ] express confidence about my abilities
- [ ] discuss job performance
- [ ] tell about my work experience
- [ ] give personal information
- [ ] inquire about job responsibilities
- [ ] provide a "work history"
- [ ] analyze successful job interview strategies

HEALTH AND EMERGENCIES

Take Exit 6 to . . .

- Report an emergency, using the present perfect tense
- Report an accident, using the present perfect tense and prepositions of location
- Ask for recommendations and locate items in a drug store
- Describe symptoms and make a doctor's appointment, using the present perfect and present perfect continuous tenses
- Ask about and give a medical history, using question formation and the present perfect tense
- Receive a doctor's medical advice, using *must*, *should*, and *might*
- Receive a pharmacist's directions for taking medication
- Offer someone medical advice, using *should* and *ought to*

Functions This Exit!

Asking for and Reporting Information
Advice-Suggestions
Obligation
Directions-Location
Possibility/Impossibility
Checking and Indicating Understanding
Asking for Repetition

Lisa is calling the police to report an emergency. What do you think Lisa and the police officer are saying to each other?

Irene isn't feeling very well. She's talking to the pharmacist at the drug store. What do you think they're saying to each other?

I Want to Report an Emergency!

A. Police.
B. I want to report an emergency!
A. Yes. Go ahead.
B. Someone has just broken* into my house.
A. Okay. What's your name?
B. Henry Wilson.
A. And the address?
B. 47 Locust Lane.
A. Telephone number?
B. What was that?[1]
A. What's your telephone number?
B. 752-1168.
A. All right. We'll send a squad car right away.
B. Thank you.

[1] What's that?
Excuse me?
What did you say?

Someone broke into *Henry Wilson's* house last night. He called the *police*. They sent a *squad car*.
Address: 47 Locust Lane
Telephone: 752-1168

1 A fire broke out in *Linda Wu's* basement yesterday. She called the *Fire Department*. They sent an *engine unit*.
Address: 94 Pine Street
Telephone: 236-5775

2 *Alexander Franklin's* mother fell* down a flight of stairs yesterday. He called the *Ajax Ambulance Service*. They sent an *ambulance*.
Address: 1471 Bedford Boulevard
Telephone: 429-3361

3 *Edith Miller's* husband had* a heart attack today. She called the *Police Emergency Unit*. They sent an *emergency medical team*.
Address: 112 Bay Avenue
Telephone: 925-8138

4 *Michael Grady's* hot water heater flooded his basement this morning. He called the *Reliable Heating Company*. They sent a *repairperson*.
Address: 20 Baker Road
Telephone: 832-7071

5 A skunk crawled into *Abigail Henderson's* house through the chimney today. She called the *ASPCA*.† They sent their *animal removal specialist*.
Address: 8 Lily Court
Telephone: 267-4004

There's been an emergency at your house. Call to report it!

* break–broke–broken
  fall–fell–fallen
  have–had–had

† ASPCA = American Society for the Prevention of Cruelty to Animals

94

What's the Word?

| an ambulance | an animal removal specialist | a squad car |
| a repairperson | an engine unit | |

1 Our telephone wires have just fallen down! — We'll send _a repairperson_ right away.

2 There's a squirrel in our basement! — We'll send _____ right away.

3 Someone has just broken into my neighbor's garage! — We'll send _____ right now.

4 A fire has just broken out in the apartment across the hall! — We'll send _____ immediately.

5 I think my grandfather has just had a heart attack! — We'll send _____ right away.

Listen

Listen and choose the correct conclusion.

1 (a.) There's a fire.
 b. Someone hurt his chin.

2 a. Someone has just broken in.
 b. His neighbor is a robber.

3 a. They have to go to the zoo right away.
 b. There's a strange noise in the fireplace.

4 a. A repairperson has to fix the dishwasher.
 b. They have to call the Fire Department.

5 a. They need to go to the post office.
 b. There's been a medical emergency.

6 a. Someone needs the police.
 b. Someone needs a mechanic.

Community Connections

With a partner, make a list of who to call in case of emergencies. Share your list with other students, compile a master list of emergency phone numbers, and give a copy to every member of the class.

I Want to Report an Accident!

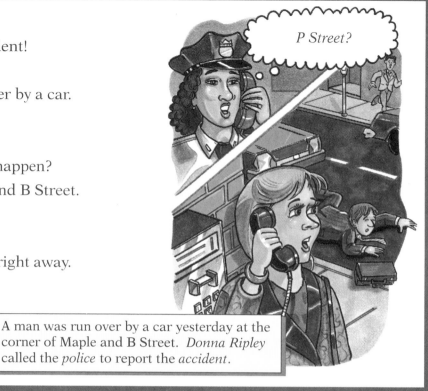

A. Police.

B. I want to report an accident!

A. Yes. Go ahead.

B. A man has been run* over by a car.

A. What's your name?

B. Donna Ripley.

A. Where did the accident happen?

B. At the corner of Maple and B Street.

A. **Did you say[1] P Street?**

B. No, "B" Street.

A. All right. We'll be there right away.

[1] Was that

A man was run over by a car yesterday at the corner of Maple and B Street. *Donna Ripley* called the *police* to report the *accident*.

1. A grocery store was robbed last night at the intersection of Harrison Road and 30th Street. *Howard Stone* called the *police* to report the *robbery*.

2. A young boy fell through the ice yesterday afternoon on the north side of Crystal Pond. *Helen Lee* called the *police* to report the *accident*.

3. An elderly couple was mugged at gunpoint yesterday evening in front of the Save-Rite Store on Fifth Street. *Miguel Rodriguez* called the *police* to report the *mugging*.

4. A tour bus overturned on the expressway this morning near Exit 17. *Brenda Watson* called the *highway patrol* to report the *accident*.

5. A spaceship full of little green people landed yesterday across the street from Charlie's Café on M Street. *Andrew Gray* called *Channel 4 News* to report the *U.F.O. landing*.

You've just witnessed an accident! Call to report it!

* run-ran-run

Fill It In!

Fill in the correct answer.

1. Someone ____ at the bus stop.
   a. has been mugged
   b. has overturned

2. Their plane has just ____.
   a. landed
   b. robbed

3. Two houses in our neighborhood ____ this week.
   a. have robbed
   b. have been robbed

4. I called the highway patrol to report the bus ____.
   a. mugging
   b. accident

5. A young boy ____ by a car!
   a. has been run over
   b. has fallen through

6. A big truck ____ on the expressway.
   a. has overturned
   b. has landed

7. Some skaters ____ through the ice at the town pond.
   a. have fallen
   b. have been robbed

8. I'm going to call ____.
   a. the U.F.O. landing
   b. Channel 7 News

Listen

Listen to the conversation and then answer true or false.

1. a. True
   b. False

2. a. True
   b. False

3. a. True
   b. False

4. a. True
   b. False

5. a. True
   b. False

6. a. True
   b. False

7. a. True
   b. False

8. a. True
   b. False

CrossTalk

Tell about an emergency experience you've had.

Have you ever had a home emergency or witnessed an accident?
When did it take place?
What happened?

Did you report it?
Who did you call?
What happened after you reported it?

Share your experience with a partner and then tell the class about it.

InterActions

With a partner or a group of students, create a reenactment of the emergency or accident situation that you experienced. Then present your "real-life" dramas to the class.

97

A. Excuse me. **Can you recommend**[1] something for a stuffy nose?

B. A stuffy nose?

A. Yes. This cold weather is really getting to me.

B. I know what you mean. Let's see . . . a stuffy nose. **I recommend**[2] Sinus-Aid Decongestant Spray.

A. Where can I find it?

B. It's in Aisle 3, on the right.

A. Thanks.

---

[1] Can you suggest

[2] I'd recommend
I suggest
I'd suggest
Try

a stuffy nose?

cold weather

Sinus-Aid Decongestant Spray

in Aisle 3, on the right

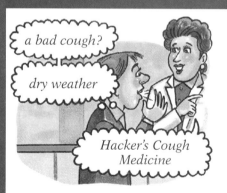

a bad cough?

dry weather

Hacker's Cough Medicine

1 in Aisle 2, halfway down on the left

itchy, watery eyes?

smog

Optimal Eyedrops

2 in Aisle 1, on the top shelf next to the toothpaste

dry skin?

freezing weather

Velveteen Lotion

3 in the last aisle, on the bottom shelf

a headache that just won't go away?

heat wave

Bynol Tablets

4 in the Cold Medicine section, next to the aspirin

frizzy hair?

humidity

Hold-It Hair Spray

5 in the front of the store, near the checkout counter

You've got a problem. Ask the pharmacist at the drug store for a recommendation.

Fill It In!

Fill in the correct answer.

1. The lotion you're looking for is _____ the hair spray.
   a. next to
   b. on

2. Lionel's Cough Medicine? You can find it over there _____ Aisle 5.
   a. in
   b. on

3. Clear-View Eyedrops? They're _____ the top shelf.
   a. up
   b. on

4. The hair spray you're looking for is right over there _____ the right.
   a. on
   b. in

5. Did you find the decongestant spray you're looking for _____ the back of the store?
   a. in
   b. on

6. Those tablets you're looking for are located _____ the eyedrops.
   a. near
   b. next

7. Lotion for dry skin is located right here _____ this section.
   a. from
   b. in

8. If we have any spray left, it's over there _____ the next aisle.
   a. in
   b. on

Listen

Listen and decide what each person's problem is.

1. This person has a problem with _____.
   a. the weather
   b. dry skin

2. This person has a problem with _____.
   a. her nose
   b. her hair

3. This person has _____.
   a. a headache
   b. frizzy hair

4. This person is unhappy about his _____.
   a. cough
   b. hair

5. This person's problem is _____.
   a. a rainy day
   b. watery eyes

6. Unfortunately, this person has _____.
   a. a bad cough
   b. dry hair

InterView

Ask ten people you know to recommend products they use to treat the following problems:

a headache   a stomachache
a sore throat   a cough
a cold   a backache

Compile a list of all the products and publish a class reference of **Recommended Medications for Common Health Problems**.

A. Doctor's office.

B. Hello. This is Gloria Hopkins calling.

A. Yes, Ms. Hopkins. What can I do for you?

B. I'm not feeling very well.

A. What seems to be the problem?

B. I have a migraine headache.

A. I see. Tell me, how long have you had a migraine headache?

B. For two days.

A. Would you like to make an appointment?

B. Yes, please.

A. Is 9:00 tomorrow morning convenient?

B. Yes. That's fine. Thank you very much.

Gloria Hopkins has had a migraine headache for two days. She's calling the *doctor's office*.

1 *Peter Johnson* has had a bad toothache since Sunday morning. He's calling the *dentist's office*.

2 *Thelma Walters* has been feeling dizzy and nauseous for the past three days. She's calling the *Riverside Clinic*.

3 *Mrs. Crawford*'s son Joey hasn't been able to move his neck since he got tackled in last Saturday's football game. Mrs. Crawford is calling the *doctor's office*.

4 *Lewis Drexell*'s right ear has been ringing for over a week. He's calling *Eye and Ear Associates*.

5 *Clara Updike*'s poodle, Fifi, has been refusing to eat her dog food since yesterday morning. Clara is calling the *Happy Pet Animal Hospital*.

You haven't been feeling well. Call the doctor's office.

What's the Answer?

1. My son hasn't ((been able to) can) sleep (since for) last Tuesday.

2. My daughter (has been has) nauseous (since for) three days.

3. My husband (isn't hasn't) been taking his medicine (since for) a week.

4. I haven't (been able to able to) move my arm (since for) last week.

5. I've (been feeling had) a terrible toothache (since for) yesterday morning.

6. Our cat (has has been) refusing to eat (since for) almost a week.

InterActions

Transform your classroom into a clinic! Everybody in the class has a role to play.

Some people are sitting in the waiting room. They're talking to each other about their ailments.

Some people are talking to the receptionist. They're explaining to the receptionist what's wrong with them.

Others are describing their symptoms to their doctors.

It's a very busy day at the clinic!

A. Well, Mr. Hutton, I think you've given me almost all the information I need for your medical history. Just one or two more questions, if that's okay.

B. Certainly.

A. Do you have any allergies?

B. No, I don't.

A. And have you ever been hospitalized?

B. No, I haven't.

A. All right, Mr. Hutton. Please take a seat. The doctor will be with you in a few minutes.

Mr. Hutton doesn't have any allergies, and he has never been hospitalized.

1 Ms. Penfield isn't on a special diet of any kind, and she has never had back trouble before.

2 Mr. Park isn't allergic to penicillin, and he has never had surgery.

3 Ms. Rivera doesn't smoke, and she has never had anesthesia before.

4 Mr. Gladstone doesn't have any history of heart disease in his family, and he has never had a bad reaction to any drugs.

5 Mrs. Schwartz doesn't have any objection to non-Western forms of medicine, and she has never had acupuncture before.

You're at the doctor's office. Give your medical history before the doctor examines you.

What's the Question?

1 <u>Is your son allergic to any medicine</u> ?

No. My son isn't allergic to any medicine.

2 _____ ?

Yes. I've had acupuncture before.

3 _____ ?

No. My daughter hasn't had anesthesia before.

4 _____ ?

Yes. You have to go on a special diet.

5 _____ ?

No. Your mother doesn't have to have surgery.

Fill It In!

Fill in the correct answer.

1 I don't have any objection to _____.
   (a.) anesthesia
   b. back trouble

2 Have you ever had a reaction to _____?
   a. allergies
   b. penicillin

3 Has your grandmother ever been _____?
   a. hospitalized
   b. acupuncture

4 We need information for your _____ history.
   a. disease
   b. medical

5 Your son has had a bad _____ to the medicine.
   a. objection
   b. reaction

6 My wife has been having _____ for a year.
   a. allergic
   b. back trouble

Cultural Intersections

What are common ways of treating medical problems in your country?

   What medicines and remedies do people use for colds, headaches, and other common problems?
Do people use herbs and other natural remedies?
Do people use acupuncture? For what ailments?

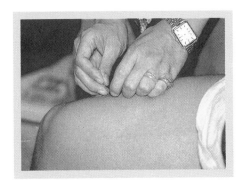

Tell about differences you have noticed between medicine in different countries.

A. I'm concerned about your blood pressure.

B. My blood pressure?

A. Yes. **I strongly advise you to**[1] change your diet.

B. Hmm. That won't be easy.

A. I know, but you really must. It's absolutely essential.

B. I understand. Do you have any suggestions that might help?

A. Yes. You should eat less salty food. And **you might**[2] look for a cookbook that has low-fat recipes.

B. Thank you. Those are good suggestions.

[1] I strongly recommend that you
I urge you to

[2] you could
it might be a good idea to

blood pressure

change your diet

eat less salty food
look for a cookbook that has low-fat recipes

weight

lose several pounds

1. start jogging
join a health club

back

begin a daily exercise routine

2. do sit-ups three times a day
take up swimming or join a yoga class

lifestyle

cut back on your workload

3. start leaving your work at the office
find a hobby that interests you

lungs

stop smoking

4. promise your family you'll quit
join an organization that helps people "kick the habit"

hearing

change your music listening habits

5. cut down on your use of those headphones
stop going to rock concerts for a while

Your doctor is concerned about your health. Listen to your doctor's advice and suggestions.

What's the Meaning?

Choose the answer that is closest in meaning.

1 *I strongly recommend that you stop.*

a. You can stop.
b. You've stopped.
ⓒ You've really got to stop.

2 *You have to.*

a. You've really had to.
b. It's necessary.
c. You should.

3 *It's essential for you to change.*

a. You've had to change.
b. You might change.
c. You really need to change.

4 *You should lose weight.*

a. You must lose weight.
b. You've been able to lose weight.
c. You ought to lose weight.

5 *I strongly advise you to cut back.*

a. You could cut back.
b. Do you think you should cut back?
c. You must cut back.

6 *It might be a good idea to start exercising.*

a. You could start exercising.
b. You must start exercising.
c. It's essential that you start exercising.

Your Turn

For Writing and Presentation

Give a short oral presentation to the class on the topic **Ten Important Ways to Stay Healthy**—your suggestions for ways to lead a healthy and productive life.

Write down on index cards the most important things you want to say. Give your presentation, but don't read it. Just use the cards to remember the important information. Use any props you wish.

Take notes on everybody's presentations. You'll probably learn some important things.

Be Sure to Follow the Directions on the Label

A. Okay. Here's your prescription.

B. Thank you.

A. Now be sure to follow the directions on the label. **You're supposed to**[1] take one tablet three times a day.

B. I understand. One tablet three times a day.

A. That's right. And one more thing. **You might**[2] feel tired after taking this medication.

B. Oh?

A. Yes, but don't worry. That's a common side effect.

B. I see. Well, thanks very much.

take 1 tablet 3 times a day

feel tired

[1] You have to	[2] You may
You've got to	You could possibly
You need to	It's possible that you'll
You must	

take 2 tablets 4 times a day

1. have a slight headache

take 1 capsule after each meal

2. feel dizzy

take 2 pills one-half hour before eating

3. lose your appetite

take 2 teaspoons as needed, but not more than 8 teaspoons in a 24-hour period

4. feel a little lightheaded

mix 1 teaspoon into your cat's food at each feeding

5. notice that your cat is very sleepy

Listen to your pharmacist's directions for taking medication.

Constructions Ahead!

| I'm |
| He's |
| She's |
| It's | supposed to do that. |
| We're |
| You're |
| They're |

1 What am I supposed to take for a headache?

You're supposed to take two aspirin.

2 Who are they supposed to call?

_____ the police.

3 Why is she supposed to have acupuncture?

_____ acupuncture because she has a backache.

4 Where is your brother going to meet us?

_____ in front of the library.

5 When does the flight from London land?

_____ in about half an hour.

6 What time should we arrive at the clinic?

_____ there by 1:30.

7 When are you supposed to return their call?

_____ right away.

What's the Word?

you ○ you've   you're   your ○ you'll

1 _You're_ supposed to take __your__ medicine now.

2 _____ got to follow the directions carefully.

3 It's possible _____ feel sleepy later.

4 _____ really ought to change your lifestyle.

5 _____ got to promise me _____ start exercising.

6 _____ might get a headache after _____ take these tablets.

7 _____ got to take _____ pills when _____ feeling dizzy.

107

Very often, we have small medical problems that aren't serious enough to require a visit to the doctor's office. Problems such as a sore throat, a stomachache, or a stuffy nose can often be taken care of with *over-the-counter* medicines available on drug store shelves. However, many people prefer to treat minor medical problems with *home remedies*. These solutions vary from country to country, from family to family, and even from person to person.

For a sore throat, it's certainly easy to stop by a local drug store and pick up a pack of lozenges. But some people prefer to make special drinks, such as warm milk with honey, or lemon juice and honey. Other people like to gargle with warm, salty water.

Stomachaches can be treated with antacids that are available at local drug stores, but many people first try drinking soda to settle their stomachs. Another more natural remedy is peppermint tea.

In addition to the various cold medicines available, many people treat their colds by having a bowl of homemade chicken soup or a clove of fresh garlic. Others like to drink hot water with lemon and honey before they go to bed.

Many books offer helpful suggestions for the treatment of minor medical problems at home and provide useful information about first-aid procedures. In case of a bee sting, for example, they recommend that you put mud or a slice of potato directly on the sting or a little vinegar on the skin so the sting will disappear.

In the case of a nose bleed, medical guides often suggest three steps in order to help stop the bleeding. First, pinch the nose. Then, tilt the head backward and rest it on the back of a chair. Finally, put an ice pack on the back of the neck. The bleeding should stop within minutes.

Modern medicine has progressed greatly in the past few years, but there are still times when it's very convenient to rely on good old *home remedies*.

True or False?

1. According to the reading, it's important to visit the doctor's office for minor medical problems.
2. It's possible to buy some medicines without going to a doctor.
3. It's esssential to drink hot water with lemon and honey when you have a cold.
4. You can find information about first-aid procedures in home medical guides.
5. It's possible to treat a bee sting with a potato.
6. It's necessary to treat medical problems with home remedies.

Do You Remember?

Try to answer these questions without looking back at the reading.

1. Lozenges and antacids are examples of _____.
   a. home remedies
   b. over-the-counter medicines
   c. first-aid procedures

2. You can treat a stomachache with _____.
   a. garlic
   b. an ice pack on the back of the neck
   c. peppermint tea

3. Home remedies are convenient to use for _____.
   a. home medical guides
   b. minor medical problems
   c. drug store shelves

4. When you want to treat a sore throat, you might want to _____.
   a. go to the drug store and buy throat lozenges
   b. make an appointment to see the doctor
   c. perform first-aid procedures

5. For nose bleeds or bee stings, it's a good idea to know _____.
   a. the names of over-the-counter medicines
   b. modern medicine
   c. a few home remedies

> **REFLECTIONS**
> Many health professionals say that a person's lifestyle and emotional well-being are important parts of a person's health. What's your opinion? Do you consider yourself a healthy person? How do you think you can improve your health?

Discuss in pairs or small groups, and then share your ideas with the class.

Your Turn

For Writing and Discussion

Complete the following and then share your remedies with a partner.

When I have a sore throat, I . . . .

When I have a stomachache, I . . . .

When I have a cold, I . . . .

When I get a bee sting, I . . . .

When I have a nose bleed, I . . . .

When I have a toothache, I . . . .

INTERCHANGE

Can I Offer a Suggestion?

A. Oh, no!

B. What's the matter?[1]

A. I have the hiccups!

B. Oh, that's too bad. Can I offer a suggestion?

A. Sure. What?

B. You should[2] blow into a paper bag.

A. You know, I've tried blowing into a paper bag when I've had the hiccups before, and that doesn't work for me. Any other suggestions?

B. Well . . . **You could**[3] hold your breath and count to twenty. That seems to work for some people.

A. Hmm. I'll give it a try. Thanks.

---

[1] What's wrong?
    What's the problem?

[2] You ought to

[3] You might _____.
    It might be a good idea to _____.
    Why don't you _____?

A. Oh, no!

B. What's the matter?[1]

A. _____!

B. Oh, that's too bad. Can I offer a suggestion?

A. Sure. What?

B. You should[2] _____.

A. You know, I've tried _____ing when _____ before, and that doesn't work for me. Any other suggestions?

B. Well . . . **You could**[3] _____. That seems to work for some people.

A. Hmm. I'll give it a try. Thanks.

Oh, no! You have a bloody nose, an upset stomach, a muscle cramp in your leg, or some other minor medical problem. Using the model dialog above as a guide, talk with a friend and get his or her advice. Feel free to adapt and expand the model any way you wish.

Matching Lines

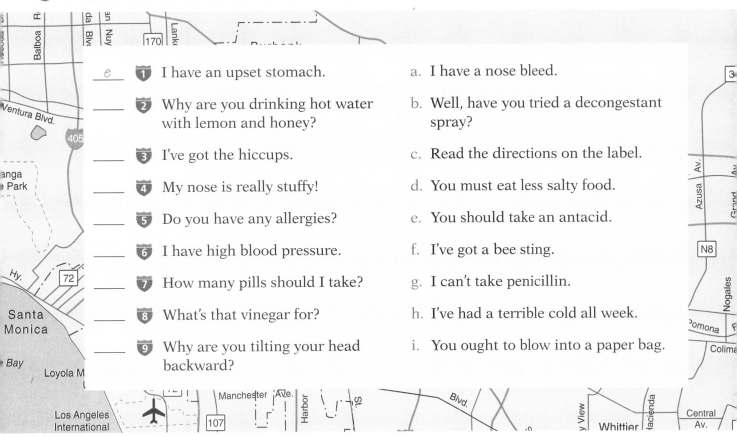

___e___ 1 I have an upset stomach.

_____ 2 Why are you drinking hot water with lemon and honey?

_____ 3 I've got the hiccups.

_____ 4 My nose is really stuffy!

_____ 5 Do you have any allergies?

_____ 6 I have high blood pressure.

_____ 7 How many pills should I take?

_____ 8 What's that vinegar for?

_____ 9 Why are you tilting your head backward?

a. I have a nose bleed.

b. Well, have you tried a decongestant spray?

c. Read the directions on the label.

d. You must eat less salty food.

e. You should take an antacid.

f. I've got a bee sting.

g. I can't take penicillin.

h. I've had a terrible cold all week.

i. You ought to blow into a paper bag.

Read the Label

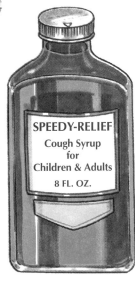

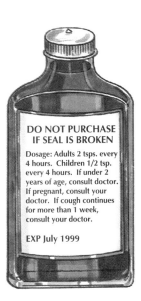

SPEEDY-RELIEF
Cough Syrup
for
Children & Adults
8 FL. OZ.

DO NOT PURCHASE
IF SEAL IS BROKEN

Dosage: Adults 2 tsps. every 4 hours. Children 1/2 tsp. every 4 hours. If under 2 years of age, consult doctor. If pregnant, consult your doctor. If cough continues for more than 1 week, consult your doctor.

EXP July 1999

1 Speedy-Relief Cough Syrup is for _____.
   a. adults only
   (b.) children and adults
   c. babies

2 If you're pregnant, you should _____.
   a. take two teaspoons every four hours
   b. take half a teaspoon every four hours
   c. talk to your doctor before taking this medicine

3 Don't buy this syrup _____.
   a. after July 1999
   b. before you break the seal
   c. unless you consult your doctor

4 You should visit the doctor if _____.
   a. you're an adult
   b. you don't understand the directions on the bottle
   c. your cough lasts longer than a week

☐ **Asking for Information**
What's the matter?
What's wrong?
What's the problem?

☐ **Asking for Advice**
Can you recommend _____?
Can you suggest _____?

☐ **Giving Advice**
You should _____.
You ought to _____.

I recommend _____.
I'd recommend _____.

I suggest _____.
I'd suggest _____.
Try _____.

You might _____.
You could _____.
It might be a good idea to _____.
Why don't you _____?

I strongly advise you to _____.
I strongly recommend that
   you _____.
I urge you to _____.

☐ **Asking for Repetition**
What was that?
What's that?
Excuse me?
What did you say?

☐ **Checking Your Understanding**
Did you say _____?
Was that _____?

☐ **Obligation**
You're supposed to _____.
You have to _____.
You've got to _____.
You need to _____.
You must _____.

☐ **Possibility**
You might _____.
You may _____.
You could possibly _____.
It's possible that you'll _____.

Now Leaving Exit 6 Construction Area

☐ **Present Perfect Tense**
☐ **Since/For**
☐ **Present Perfect Continuous Tense**
☐ **Prepositions of Location**
☐ **Question Formation**
☐ **Supposed to**

Sorry for the inconvenience. For more information see pages 166 and 167.

ExpressWays Checklist

I can . . .

☐ Report an emergency
☐ Report an accident
☐ Ask for recommendations and locate items in a drug store
☐ Describe symptoms and make a doctor's appointment
☐ Ask about and give a medical history
☐ Receive a doctor's medical advice
☐ Receive a pharmacist's directions for taking medication
☐ Offer someone medical advice

REST STOP

Take a break!
Have a conversation!

Here are some scenes from Exits 4, 5, and 6.

Who do you think these people are?
What do you think they're talking about?

In pairs or small groups, create conversations based on these scenes and act them out.

Exit 7

SHOPPING

Take Exit 7 to . . .

➤ Locate items in a department store, using prepositions of location

➤ Select an item in a store, using *one/ones*

➤ Ask for articles of clothing in a store, using adjectives

➤ Return items to a department store, using adjectives, *too*, and comparatives

➤ Access the services of a post office, using passives and *will*

➤ Discuss features of products

Functions This Exit!

Want-Desire
Asking for and Reporting
    Information
Offering to Help
Directions-Location
Requests
Regret
Asking for Repetition
Satisfaction/Dissatisfaction
Checking and Indicating
    Understanding
Hesitating

Roy is looking for something in a department store. What do you think Roy and the salesperson are saying to each other?

Ann wants to mail a package at the post office. What do you think Ann and the postal clerk are saying to each other?

Where Can I Find Washing Machines?

A. Excuse me. **Where can I find**[1] washing machines?

B. Washing machines? They're in the Household Appliances Department in the basement.

A. In the basement? I see. **Could you tell me**[2] how to get there?

B. Sure. Take the escalator over there down one floor.

A. Thanks very much.

> [1] Where are _____?
> Where are _____ located?
>
> [2] Can you tell me

washing machines?

Household Appliances Department in the basement

Take the escalator over there down one floor.

neckties?

Men's Clothing Department on the 2nd floor

1 There's an elevator near the main entrance to the store.

pots and pans?

Housewares Department on the 3rd floor

2 Walk up this staircase one flight and you'll be on "3."

bedroom sets?

Furniture Department at the rear of the store

3 Walk down this aisle past Women's Clothing, and you'll see Furniture on the right in the corner.

videocassette recorders?

Home Entertainment Department on the ground level

4 Walk down the steps over there two flights, or if you prefer, take the elevator.

designer jeans for kids?

Children's Clothing Department near the side entrance

5 Walk down that way until you come to the snack bar, and you'll see Children's Clothing on the left.

You need directions in a department store.

ExpressWays

STORE DIRECTORY

Children's Clothing	2
Customer Service	7
Furniture	1
Home Entertainment	3
Household Appliances	6
Housewares	B
Men's Clothing	4
Women's Clothing	5

1. You can find beds in the __Furniture__ Department on the __first__ floor.

2. Microwave ovens are in the _____ Department on the _____ floor.

3. You'll find stereos in the _____ Department. Take the escalator to the _____ floor.

4. Pots and pans are in the _____ Department in the _____.

5. Girls' coats? They're in the _____ Department on the _____ floor.

6. You need to get a dress for your friend's wedding? The _____ Department is on the _____ floor.

7. A tie for your father? Try the _____ Department on the _____ floor.

8. You want to return that pan? _____ is on the _____ floor.

Listen

Listen and complete the sentence.

1. (a.) the entrance
   b. the right

2. a. the third floor
   b. up

3. a. the basement
   b. the fourth floor

4. a. rear
   b. building

5. a. the basement
   b. the escalator

6. a. side entrance
   b. left

Figure It Out!

Think of a department store item, tell where you can buy it, and see if others can guess the item.

I'm thinking of something you can buy in the Housewares Department.

A. May I help you?[1]

B. Yes. **I'd like to**[2] buy a Sony color TV.

A. Hmm. We carry Sony color TVs in several different models. Which one are you interested in?

B. I'd like the one with the 25-inch screen and remote control.

A. All right. Let me see if that's in stock. I'll be right back.

[1] Can I help you?

[2] I want to

a Sony color TV

with the 25-inch screen and remote control

a General Electric gas range

1 with the self-cleaning oven

a Westinghouse refrigerator

2 with an automatic ice maker

a Casio watch

3 that's also a calculator

a Norelco coffeemaker

4 that makes 12 cups and beeps when the coffee is ready

an IBM Personal Computer

5 with 16 megabytes of memory

You're looking for a particular item in a department store.

What's the Word?

| TV ∘ computer refrigerator gas range coffeemaker ∘ watch |

1. I'd like to buy a _refrigerator_ with an automatic ice maker.

2. I'd like to look at the _____ that makes twenty cups.

3. We're interested in a _____ with remote control.

4. Do you have a personal _____ at home?

5. I'd like to buy a waterproof _____.

6. Is this the _____ with a self-cleaning oven?

Listen

Listen to the conversation. What are these people talking about?

1. a. a TV ✓
   b. a window

2. a. a watch
   b. a coffeemaker

3. a. a computer
   b. a refrigerator

4. a. a car
   b. a gas range

5. a. a sofa
   b. a salesperson

6. a. a clock
   b. a computer

7. a. a VCR
   b. an ice maker

8. a. an oven
   b. a washing machine

CrossTalk

When you buy a refrigerator, you should buy one with . . . .

If you want to buy a TV, I recommend one that has . . . .

If you're looking for a computer, you should definitely get one with . . . .

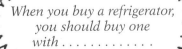

What features should you look for when you're making an important purchase such as a refrigerator, a television set, or a computer? Talk with a partner and then share your consumer advice with the class.

A. Excuse me. **Could you help me?**[1]

B. **Certainly.**[2] What can I do for you?

A. I'm looking for a leather belt for my husband.

B. What size does he wear?

A. Size 36 . . . I think.

B. What color would you like?

A. Dark brown, if you have it.

B. Okay. Let's see . . . a size 36 dark brown leather belt. Do you think your husband will like this one?

A. Yes. I'm sure he will. I'll take it.

B. Will this be cash or charge?

A. Do you take MasterCard?

B. No, I'm afraid not. We only accept our own store credit card.

A. Oh. In that case, I'll pay cash.

[1] Can you help me?   [2] Of course.
                              I'd be happy to.
                              I'd be glad to.

a leather belt
my husband
size 36
dark brown

MasterCard?

a V-neck sweater
my sister
small
beige

 1 Visa?

a permanent
  press dress shirt
my son
size 15
light blue

2 the Diner's Club card?

a sleeveless blouse
my girlfriend
medium
bright red

3 the Discover Card?

sneakers
my daughter
size 8
white

4 a personal check?

a jogging suit
my boyfriend
large
red, white, and blue

5 the American Express card?

You want to buy somebody something in a department store.

Constructions Ahead!

a	size 36	dark brown	leather	belt
a	small	black	plastic	purse
a	large	Sony	color	TV

1 I'm looking for a ____.
    a. blue light skirt
    (b.) light blue skirt
    c. skirt light blue

2 My daughter needs a pair of ____.
    a. size one sneakers pink
    b. pink sneakers size one
    c. size one pink sneakers

3 My wife bought me a ____.
    a. white shirt permanent press
    b. white permanent press shirt
    c. shirt white permanent press

4 I'll take this ____.
    a. large sweater light green
    b. light green large sweater
    c. large light green sweater

5 I'd like the ____.
    a. small RCA color TV
    b. color RCA small TV
    c. small color TV RCA

6 I'm trying to find a ____.
    a. necktie red bright
    b. bright red necktie
    c. red bright necktie

Listen

Listen to the conversation. What word do you hear?

1 (a.) size 34
    b. size 44

2 a. 15-33
    b. 16-33

3 a. like
    b. light

4 a. shirt
    b. medium

5 a. small
    b. 11

6 a. white
    b. bright

7 a. charge
    b. large

8 a. pink
    b. size 12

9 a. mother
    b. brother

10 a. size 32
    b. black

11 a. dress
    b. shirt

12 a. credit card
    b. MasterCard

CrossTalk

Talk with a partner about how you pay for things you buy.

Do you prefer to pay for things in cash, with a check, or with a credit card?

What are the advantages and disadvantages of each?

How do people in your country usually pay for their purchases?

Tell the class about your discussion. Which method of payment is the most common?

I'd Like to Return This Coat

coat
lightweight
heavy

pajamas
long
short

A. **I'd like to**[1] return this coat.
B. All right. Do you have the receipt?
A. Yes. Here you are.
B. **May I ask**[2] why you're returning it?
A. Yes. It's too lightweight.
B. **Would you like to**[3] exchange it for a heavier one?
A. No, I don't think so. I'd just like a refund, please.
B. Certainly.

A. **I'd like to**[1] return these pajamas.
B. All right. Do you have the receipt?
A. Yes. Here you are.
B. **May I ask**[2] why you're returning them?
A. Yes. They're too long.
B. **Would you like to**[3] exchange them for some shorter ones?
A. No, I don't think so. I'd just like a refund, please.
B. Certainly.

[1] I want to

[2] Can I ask
Could I ask

[3] Do you want to
[more formal]
Would you care to

1 necktie
fancy
conservative

2 earrings
big
small

3 jeans
tight
large

4 jigsaw puzzle
simple
difficult

5 walkie-talkie set
weak
powerful

You'd like to return something in a department store.

What's the Answer?

1. These gloves are too tight. I think I'd like to try a (smaller (bigger)) pair.

2. I want to exchange this puzzle for one that's more difficult. This is too (simpler   easy).

3. This suitcase is a little too heavy. I'd like one that's more (difficult   lightweight).

4. This vest is too long. I'd like one a little (taller   shorter).

5. This shortwave radio is very weak. I'd like one that's (simpler   more powerful).

6. This tie is too fancy. I'd like one that's more (lightweight   conservative).

Listen

Listen and choose the best answer.

1. (a.) It's too heavy.
   b. It's too weak.

2. a. It's difficult.
   b. It's easy to follow.

3. a. The rug is too big.
   b. The rug is too small.

4. a. She needs more comfortable ones.
   b. She needs more powerful ones.

5. a. He doesn't want a fancy one.
   b. He wants a fancier one.

6. a. She wants a shorter one.
   b. She wants a longer one.

7. a. She wants a darker one.
   b. She wants a lighter one.

8. a. It was too simple.
   b. It was too difficult.

InterActions

When the people on page 122 asked for a refund, the clerk replied:

But what if the clerk at the Customer Service Counter replied:

Certainly.

Sorry. We don't give refunds.

What would happen next? With a partner, choose one of the situations on page 122 and create a different ending to the scene. Role-play the scene for the class and discuss the situation with other students.

123

Shoppers in the United States have many different retail stores to choose from. They can shop at large department stores, furniture stores, jewelry stores, electronic equipment stores, clothing boutiques, and many others. Another type of retail store, the catalog store, has become popular with U.S. consumers.

Catalog stores offer much of the same merchandise as conventional retail stores. However, in these stores, shoppers select the items they wish to buy from large catalogs that are filled with photographs and descriptions of all the different merchandise. The variety of products listed in the catalogs includes everything from appliances and baby clothing to video equipment and watches. The prices of these items are comparatively low. In fact, the same items often cost more in other retail stores. And that's the reason many people prefer to shop in catalog stores.

When shoppers go to a catalog store, they see many brand-name products on display. If they are interested in purchasing an item, they need to follow this simple procedure.

- First, they go to a counter to find the store's catalog.
- They look in the catalog to find the exact item they wish to buy.
- Then, they fill out an order form with the name of the item, the item number from the catalog, the price, and their name and address.
- After completing the form, the customer gives it to a salesperson, who checks to see if the item is in stock.
- If the item is available, the stockroom sends it on a conveyor belt to the pick-up counter. When the item arrives at the pick-up counter, the customer's name is called, and the customer pays for the item.

The whole procedure usually takes ten to twenty minutes. If the item isn't available, the salesperson can usually check the store's computer and find out when it will be in stock again.

Catalog stores usually don't offer all the services that regular retail stores do. They usually don't have very many salespeople, so customers can't expect to receive much assistance or attention from store employees. Customers need to know about the features and the quality of the items they wish to buy before they shop, since there isn't much opportunity to ask questions or examine the products in the store. However, catalog stores offer quality items at lower prices, and consumers seem to appreciate this.

True or False?

1. A catalog store is a type of retail store.
2. The items in catalog stores often cost more than items at other stores.
3. In catalog stores, customers have to fill out order forms to purchase items.
4. Customers at catalog stores use the store's computer to check the availability of items.
5. Catalog stores are probably popular because the services they offer are excellent.

What's the Answer?

1. *Consumers* are ____.
   a. salespeople
   b. shoppers *(circled)*
   c. services

2. Another word for *merchandise* is ____.
   a. products
   b. photographs
   c. clothing

3. *In stock* means ____.
   a. in the catalog
   b. at the pick-up counter
   c. available

4. At a catalog store, the customer finds the item number ____.
   a. on the order form
   b. at the pick-up counter
   c. in the catalog

5. The most important idea of the reading is that catalog stores ____.
   a. offer quality merchandise at lower prices
   b. are more popular than conventional retail stores
   c. offer the exact item the customer wishes to purchase

Cultural Intersections

Are there catalog stores in your country? Tell about different kinds of stores where you live.

Survey

Take a survey of students in your class and other people you know. Decide on a few products and ask people's opinions about the best places to buy these products. For example:

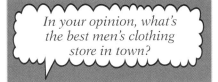

In your opinion, what's the best place to buy furniture?

In your opinion, what's the best men's clothing store in town?

In your opinion, what's the best store for household appliances?

I'm looking for a computer. In your opinion, what's the best place to buy one?

Report your findings to the class. Create a **Community Shopping Guide** based on everybody's surveys.

A. I'd like to purchase a money order, please.

B. **I'm sorry.**[1] You've got the wrong window. Money orders can be purchased at Window Number 3.

A. **Did you say**[2] Window Number 3?

B. Yes, that's right.

A. Thanks very much.

[1] Sorry.

[2] Was that

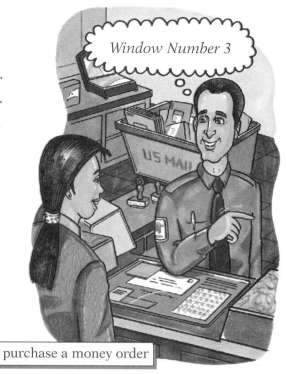

Window Number 3

purchase a money order

Window Number 1

1 buy some stamps

the next window

2 send* a registered letter

the window on the left

3 file a change of address form

Window Number 2

4 apply for a post office box

the other window

5 mail some packages

You're at the post office.

* send-sent-sent

Constructions Ahead!

mail a letter	— letters can be mailed
buy a ticket	— tickets can be bought
get a license	— licenses can be gotten
see a film	— films can be seen
take a photo	— photos can be taken

1 I want to send this package to Boston.

Packages _can be sent_ over there.

2 I need to buy a ticket for the next flight to Mexico City.

Tickets _____ at the next counter.

3 Can I return this shirt?

Shirts _____ within ten days.

4 We'd like to see the apartment that's for rent on Bayside Boulevard.

The apartment _____ this afternoon.

5 When can I pick up the cake that I ordered?

Your cake _____ after 8:00 A.M.

6 Should I take the medicine before meals?

The medicine _____ before or after meals.

Fill It In!

Fill in the correct answer.

1 I need to get a ____ because I'm moving.
   a. registered letter
   (b.) change of address form
   c. money order

2 I'd like to ____ a money order.
   a. file
   b. apply for
   c. buy

3 I have to get my mail from the ____.
   a. post office box
   b. first class stamps
   c. new forms

4 Stamps can be gotten at the next ____.
   a. Window Number 3
   b. post office box
   c. window

5 Where can stamps be ____?
   a. filed
   b. purchased
   c. applied for

6 This ____ can be filled out over there.
   a. form
   b. box
   c. letter

Community Connections

Visit your local post office and find out the cost of the following:

a book of stamps   an aerogramme
a roll of stamps   a registered letter
a postcard   a money order

Report your findings to the class.

I'd Like to Mail This Package to Minneapolis

A. I'd like to mail this package to Minneapolis.

B. How would you like to send it?

A. First class, please.

B. Okay. **Let's see.**[1] It's twelve pounds, so that'll be ten dollars and eighty-one cents.

A. Ten eighty-one?

B. Yes. That's a pretty heavy package you've got there.

A. Hmm. **I guess**[2] it is. It's a crystal punch bowl I'm sending to my Aunt Helen.

B. Well, it can be sent parcel post, if you want.

A. How long will that take?

B. About twelve days.

A. And how much will it cost?

B. **Let's see.**[1] Twelve pounds . . . to Minneapolis. That'll cost five ninety-four.

A. Okay. I'll send it parcel post.

---

[1] Let me see. [2] I suppose
Let's see now.

Minneapolis

12 lbs.
$10.81

about 12 days
$5.94

crystal punch bowl
my Aunt Helen

San Francisco

13 lbs.
$15.73

around 14 days
$12.78

1 wedding gift
my college roommate

Birmingham, Alabama

15 lbs.
$12.86

about a week
$6.54

2 electric train set
my niece and nephew

West Point, New York

7 lbs.
$5.58

7 to 10 days
$3.19

3 toaster oven
my son at the military
academy

Salt Lake City

10 lbs.
$11.45

10 to 14 days
$8.07

4 unabridged dictionary
my daughter in graduate
school

Trenton, New Jersey

20 lbs.
$11.09

6 or 7 days
$4.43

5 bowling ball
my Uncle Ted

You'd like to mail
a package at the
post office.

Crossed Lines

Put the following lines in the correct order.

____ Will it take longer to get there?

____ Yes. That's what it'll cost to send it first class.

____ Let me see. It's fifteen pounds, so that'll be sixteen ninety-five.

____ Oh, yes. Parcel post . . . to Pittsburgh. That would be nine eighty.

_1_ I'd like to mail this package to Pittsburgh.

____ A week? Hmm. I think I'd better send it first class. It's a birthday gift for my Cousin Charlie, and his birthday is this Thursday.

____ How would you like to send it?

____ Yes. It'll take about a week.

____ If you send it first class, I'm sure your Cousin Charlie will get his birthday gift by this Thursday.

____ Sixteen ninety-five?

____ Would it be cheaper to send it parcel post?

____ First class, please.

Listen

Listen and choose the correct number.

1. a. 10 (circled)
   b. 12

2. a. $20.96
   b. $12.96

3. a. seven
   b. eleven

4. a. $14.68
   b. $40.68

5. a. five
   b. nine

6. a. four
   b. fourteen

7. a. $13.78
   b. $15.78

8. a. $10.64
   b. $12.64

Your Turn

For Writing and Discussion

Make a list of all the presents you're going to give to friends and family members this year. If you're going to mail the presents, decide if you're going to send them first class or parcel post.

INTERCHANGE

I'm Interested in This Car

A. Can I help you?

B. Yes. I'm interested in this car.

A. You have very good taste. This is one of the finest cars we have.

B. Really?

A. Yes. Let me point out some of its special features.

B. Okay.

A. First, notice that the controls on the dashboard are all computerized.

B. Hmm. I see that.

A. Also, the seat fully reclines so that your passenger can sleep during those long trips.

B. That's a very nice feature.

A. And I should also point out that an AM-FM stereo radio with CD player is included.

B. Oh. That's very interesting. Can I ask how much it costs?

A. Certainly. This particular car costs $20,000, and let me mention that we offer a very good installment plan to help you spread out the payments.

B. I see.

A. Would you like me to write up an order slip for you?

B. Uh . . . not right now, thanks. I want to shop around a little more before I make a decision.

A. Can I help you?

B. Yes. I'm interested in this _____.

A. You have very good taste. This is one of the finest _____s we have.

B. Really?

A. Yes. Let me point out some of its special features.

B. Okay.

A. First, notice that _____
_____.

B. Hmm. I see that.

A. Also, _____
_____.

B. That's a very nice feature.

A. And I should also point out that _____
_____.

B. Oh. That's very interesting. Can I ask how much it costs?

A. Certainly. This particular _____ costs _____,
and let me mention that we offer a very good installment plan to help you spread
out the payments.

B. I see.

A. Would you like me to write up an order slip for you?

B. Uh . . . not right now, thanks. I want to shop around a little more before I make
a decision.

You're planning to make a major purchase such as a washing machine, a stove, a stereo system,
a hot tub, or even a yacht! Create a conversation with a salesperson, using the model dialog
above as a guide. Feel free to adapt and expand the model any way you wish.

Your Turn

For Writing and Discussion

Tell about your favorite possession. Perhaps it's a necklace
or a watch. Maybe it's your car, or a special gift you
once received.

How long have you had it?
Did you buy it yourself or did someone
give it to you?
Why is it special to you?

If it isn't too valuable, bring it to class to show other students.
Otherwise, bring in a photograph or describe it.

Looking Back

Asking about Location
Where can I find _____?
Where are _____?
Where are _____ located?

Asking for Information
Could you tell me _____?
Can you tell me _____?

May I ask _____?
Can I ask _____?
Could I ask _____?

Offering to Help
May I help you?
Can I help you?

Want-Desire
Would you like to _____?
Do you want to _____?
[more formal]
Would you care to _____?

I'd like to _____.
I want to _____.

Requests
Could you help me?
Can you help me?

Responding to Requests
Certainly.
Of course.
I'd be happy to.
I'd be glad to.

Regret
I'm sorry.
Sorry.

Asking for Repetition
Did you say _____?
Was that _____?

Hesitating
Let's see.
Let me see.
Let's see now.

Now Leaving Exit 7 Construction Area

☐ **Prepositions of Location**
☐ **Adjectives**
☐ **Too**
☐ **Comparatives**
☐ **One/Ones**
☐ **Future: Will**
☐ **Singular/Plural**
☐ **Passives: Introduction**

Sorry for the inconvenience. For more information see pages 168 and 169.

ExpressWays Checklist
I can . . .

☐ Locate items in a department store
☐ Select items in a store
☐ Ask for articles of clothing in a store
☐ Return items to a department store
☐ Access the services of a post office
☐ Discuss features of products

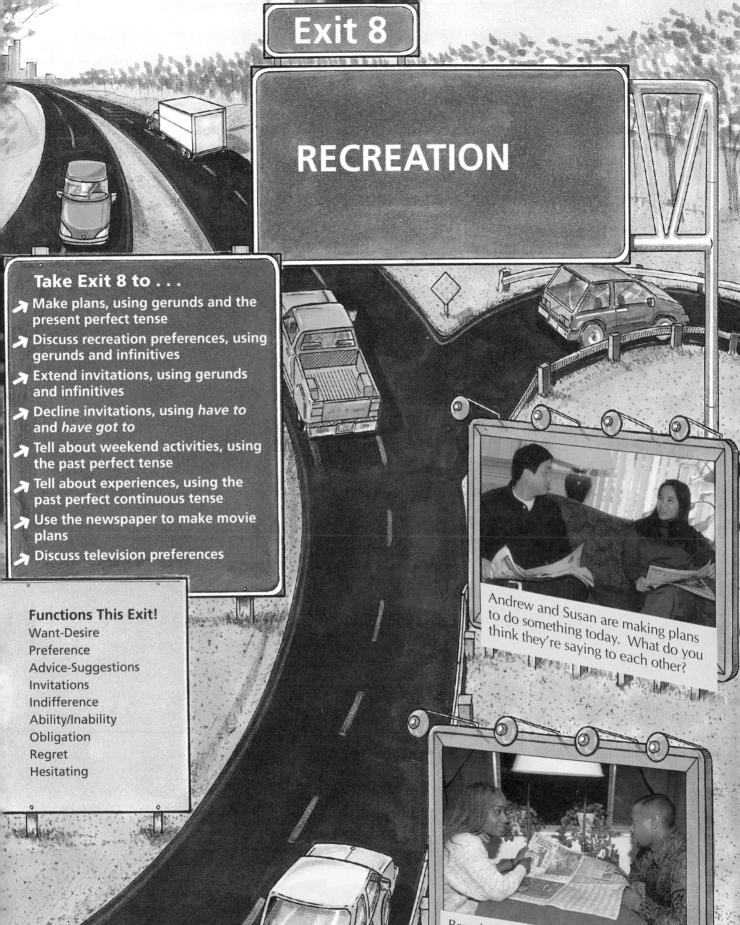

Exit 8

RECREATION

Take Exit 8 to . . .

➔ Make plans, using gerunds and the present perfect tense

➔ Discuss recreation preferences, using gerunds and infinitives

➔ Extend invitations, using gerunds and infinitives

➔ Decline invitations, using *have to* and *have got to*

➔ Tell about weekend activities, using the past perfect tense

➔ Tell about experiences, using the past perfect continuous tense

➔ Use the newspaper to make movie plans

➔ Discuss television preferences

Functions This Exit!

Want-Desire
Preference
Advice-Suggestions
Invitations
Indifference
Ability/Inability
Obligation
Regret
Hesitating

Andrew and Susan are making plans to do something today. What do you think they're saying to each other?

Brenda and Roland are trying to decide what movie to see. What do you think they're saying to each other?

A. What do you want to do today?

B. I don't know. Do you have any suggestions?

A. How about[1] going to the ballgame?

B. Hmm. **I don't really feel like[2]** going to the ballgame. Any other ideas?

A. Well, **how about[1]** seeing a movie?

B. **Good idea![3]** We haven't seen a movie in a long time.

---

[1] What about

[2] I don't really feel like ____ing.
I'm not really in the mood to ____.

[3] Good suggestion!

Make plans for the day with a friend.

Constructions Ahead!

I don't want to	{ play tennis. go to the movies. have a picnic.
I don't feel like	{ playing tennis. going to the movies. having a picnic.

drive   go   play   see   do

Do you want to _____go_____ 1 swimming?

No, I don't feel like _____ 2 swimming today.

How about _____ 3 to the mountains?

No, I'm not really in the mood to _____ 4 anywhere.

What about a movie? Would you like to _____ 5 *The Shark*?

No, I really don't want to _____ 6 a movie.

Do you feel like _____ 7 soccer?

No, I don't want to _____ 8 soccer.

Well, what do you want to _____ 9 ?

I guess I don't feel like _____ 10 anything!

CrossTalk

Circulate around the room. Talk with other students about suggestions for fun weekend activities.

> Let's get together this weekend. Do you have any suggestions?

> How about seeing a movie?

> I'm in the mood to go dancing.

Then discuss all the suggestions as a class. Which suggestion does everybody like the best? Make plans to get together as a class and do this activity on a future weekend.

What Would You Prefer to Do?

A. Let's¹ go swimming today!

B. Good idea. Where do you want to go?

A. Oh, I don't know. How about going to the town pool? Or we could always swim at the lake.

B. **It doesn't make any difference to me.²** What would you **prefer to³** do?

A. I think I'd **prefer to³** go to the town pool.

B. Okay. That's fine with me.

¹ Let's _____!
Why don't we _____?

² It doesn't matter to me.
I don't care.

³ rather

go to the town pool
swim at the lake

1 go to the rink
skate on the pond

2 go for a hike
ride our bikes

3 see the new Disney film
see the new James Bond movie

4 go to the Science Museum
visit the Museum of Natural History

5 play hopscotch
play "hide and seek"

Express your preference when making plans for the day.

136

What's the Answer?

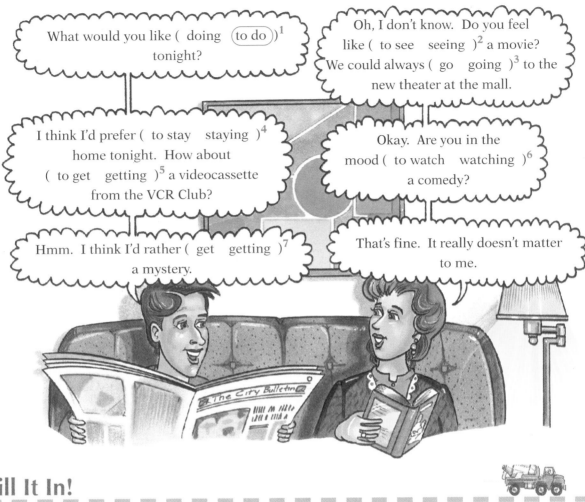

What would you like (doing (to do))[1] tonight?

Oh, I don't know. Do you feel like (to see seeing)[2] a movie? We could always (go going)[3] to the new theater at the mall.

I think I'd prefer (to stay staying)[4] home tonight. How about (to get getting)[5] a videocassette from the VCR Club?

Okay. Are you in the mood (to watch watching)[6] a comedy?

Hmm. I think I'd rather (get getting)[7] a mystery.

That's fine. It really doesn't matter to me.

Fill It In!

Fill in the correct answer.

1 Why don't we go for a bike ____?
   a. hike
   b. ride *(circled)*

2 We could play "hide and ____."
   a. see
   b. seek

3 How about swimming ____?
   a. to the pool
   b. at the pool

4 I'd rather ____ hopscotch.
   a. prefer
   b. play

5 I'd like to ____ a museum.
   a. go to
   b. do

6 Let's go skating ____.
   a. on the lake
   b. at the pool

7 What about ____ our bikes?
   a. hiking
   b. riding

8 We've just seen an adventure ____.
   a. museum
   b. film

Survey

Take a survey of ten people of different ages — children, teenagers, young adults, middle-aged adults, and senior citizens. Ask people about their favorite weekend activities. Report the results to the class. What differences are there based on people's ages?

Would You Like to Go Skiing Tomorrow?

A. **Would you like to**[1] go skiing tomorrow?

B. **That sounds great.**[2] I haven't gone skiing in a long time. But wait a minute! Isn't it supposed to be very warm tomorrow?

A. Gee. I hadn't heard that.

B. I'm pretty sure it's supposed to be very warm. I heard it on the radio.

A. In that case, going skiing probably wouldn't be a very good idea.

B. Hmm. I guess you're right.

A. Let's wait and see what the weather is like tomorrow.

B. Okay. I'll call you in the morning.

---

[1] How would you like to ____?
Do you want to ____?
Would you be interested in ____ing?

[2] That sounds like fun.
I'd love to.
I'd like to.

I heard it on the radio.

🛡️1 I read it in the paper.

🛡️2 I saw the forecast on TV this morning.

🛡️3 The weather forecaster on Channel 4 predicted it.

🛡️4 They said so on the morning news.

🛡️5 The cashier at the drug store told me.

Invite someone to do something tomorrow, but don't forget about the weather!

Fill It In!

1. I'd like to play football, but my parents think that ___playing___ soccer is a better idea.

2. My daughter really wants to take ballet lessons, but _____ lessons from a professional is so expensive!

3. We'd like to go sailing, but _____ sailing with the kids wouldn't be a very good idea.

4. I'd really like to drive that sports car, but _____ a car with a manual transmission is too difficult for me.

5. Timmy and Susie want to ride their bikes near the interstate, but I told them that _____ near a highway is too dangerous.

6. My teenage daughters want to hang out at the shopping mall, but I think _____ out at the mall isn't a very good idea. What do you think?

7.

I really like to drink coffee in the morning, but _____ more than one cup makes me very nervous.

Listen

Listen and decide which weather forecast is correct.

1. a. It's supposed to be clear this afternoon.
   b. It's supposed to rain.

2. a. It's 45 degrees right now.
   b. It's 30 degrees right now.

3. a. It's supposed to snow this morning.
   b. It's supposed to rain this morning.

4. a. It'll be in the 80s tonight.
   b. It'll be in the 70s tonight.

5. a. It's supposed to be foggy.
   b. It's supposed to rain in the area.

6. a. It's going to be sunny today.
   b. It's going to be windy today.

Your Turn

For Writing and Discussion

How are you affected by the weather?

What's your favorite kind of weather? Why?
How do you feel on those kinds of days?
What activities do you enjoy doing?

What's your least favorite kind of weather?
How do you feel when the weather is like that?
What activities do you like to do to make you feel better?

A. Would you by any chance be interested in[1] going dancing tomorrow night?

B. Tomorrow night? I'm afraid **I can't.**[2] **I have to**[3] work overtime.

A. That's too bad.

B. It is. Going dancing sounds like a lot more fun than working overtime. Maybe some other time.

[1] Would you by any chance be
    interested in ___ing?
How would you like to ___?
Do you want to ___?

[2] I won't be able to

[3] I've got to
I'm supposed to

go dancing tomorrow night?

work overtime

see a movie this weekend?

finish a term paper

1

go out for dinner tonight?

attend a business meeting

2

go to a concert this Saturday evening?

take care of my sister's children

3

see a play next Sunday?

work on my taxes

4

go roller skating this Saturday afternoon?

help my parents clean up the yard

5

You invite a friend to do something, but the person refuses.

Fill It In!

Fill in the correct answer.

1. How would you like ____?
   a. go swimming
   b. (to go swimming)
   c. swimming

2. Are you in the mood ____?
   a. to dance
   b. dancing
   c. dance

3. I'm interested in ____.
   a. skiing
   b. to ski
   c. to going skiing

4. I'd prefer ____ the bus.
   a. take
   b. to take
   c. taking

5. How about ____ outdoors?
   a. play
   b. to play
   c. playing

6. We're supposed ____ for a test.
   a. studying
   b. to study
   c. study

7. George didn't feel like ____.
   a. left
   b. to leave
   c. leaving

8. They'd rather ____.
   a. to go sailing
   b. going sailing
   c. go sailing

Listen

Listen and decide whether someone accepted or rejected the other person's invitation.

1. a. accepted
   b. rejected

2. a. accepted
   b. rejected

3. a. accepted
   b. rejected

4. a. accepted
   b. rejected

5. a. accepted
   b. rejected

6. a. accepted
   b. rejected

7. a. accepted
   b. rejected

8. a. accepted
   b. rejected

CrossTalk

Have you ever invited somebody to do something and the person refused you?

How did you feel?
Did you believe the person's excuse?
Did you invite the person to do something another time?
Did the person accept your second invitation, or give you another excuse?

Talk with a partner. Then share your stories with the class.

A. What did you do over the weekend?

B. I saw a play.

A. Did you enjoy it?

B. Yes. I hadn't seen a play in ages! How about you? What did YOU do over the weekend?

A. I went sailing.

B. Hmm. Didn't you go sailing the weekend before?

A. Yes, I did. And I had gone sailing the weekend before THAT, too!

B. Boy, you really enjoy going sailing!

A. I sure do! I like to go sailing whenever I can.

see a play
go sailing

1 work in my garden
drive to the mountains

2 take my children
to the zoo
write letters

3 fly my kite
wash my car

4 read a novel
go dancing

5 cook and bake
volunteer at the
nursing home

Talk with a friend about what you did over the weekend.

Constructions Ahead!

I
He
She
It	} had/hadn't gone.
We
You
They

1 Why didn't Bob go skiing with us last weekend?

He ___had gone___ skiing the weekend before.

2 Why didn't the Thompsons play bridge with us last night?

They _____ bridge the night before.

3 Carmen really enjoyed riding her bicycle yesterday.

I know. She _____ her bicycle in ages.

4 Did you enjoy seeing that James Bond film the other night?

Yes. I _____ a good adventure movie in a long time.

5 Why did Peter look so upset when I saw him the other day?

He _____ a long letter to his girlfriend the week before, and she _____ written back to him.

6 Is it true that you and your brother fell several times when you went ice skating the other day?

Yes, it's true. That's because we _____ ice skating in a long time.

Figure It Out!

Write a short description of a wonderful weekend you had. Tell all the things you did and why you enjoyed doing them. Give your description to your teacher. Your teacher will "mix up" everybody's descriptions and hand them to other students in the class. Then interview other students, ask them questions, and find out whose description you have.

A. Tell me, how did your parents enjoy their vacation in Florida?

B. They were really disappointed. The weather was miserable, and the hotel was crowded.

A. **That's a shame!**[1] They had been looking forward to their vacation in Florida for a long time.

B. I know. They had been talking about it for weeks!

[1] That's too bad!
What a shame!
What a pity!

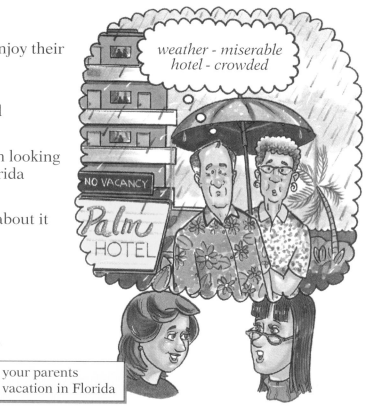

weather - miserable
hotel - crowded

your parents
vacation in Florida

food - cold
service - slow

1 your sister
dinner at The Ritz

weather - warm
ski lifts - expensive

2 your brother
ski vacation

plane ride - bumpy
movie - boring

3 you
flight to San Francisco

water - choppy
cabins - tiny

4 you and your wife
cruise to the Bahamas

band - old-fashioned
deejay - bad

5 you
Senior Prom

Tell about a disappointing experience.

144

Constructions Ahead!

> I
> He
> She
> It
> We
> You
> They
> } had been working.

1 I really enjoyed my vacation in Spain. I *(plan)* <u>had been planning</u> it for months.

2 Rita enjoyed seeing her relatives from San Antonio. She *(want)* _____ to see them for a long time.

3 I was very disappointed in that new Italian restaurant. All my friends *(tell)* _____ me how good the food is, but I disagree.

4 When Alice and Tom announced their engagement last week, nobody was surprised. Everybody *(expect)* _____ it for weeks!

5 David was very disappointed. He *(hope)* _____ to get a promotion at work, but he didn't get it.

6 My husband and I really enjoyed our cruise to South America. We *(look forward)* _____ to it all year.

7 Jane, I'm so happy you enjoyed your trip to Australia. You *(talk)* _____ about going there since your daughter moved to Sydney last year.

8 We weren't surprised when our dishwasher finally stopped working. It *(leak)* _____ for several weeks!

Your Turn

For Writing and Discussion

Tell about something special you had been looking forward to. Perhaps it was a trip to a place you had always wanted to see. Or perhaps it was a special birthday celebration or anniversary.

How long had you been looking forward to it?

What had you done beforehand to plan for it?

How did it turn out? Were you disappointed, or was it as wonderful as you had hoped?

145

A. Would you like to see a movie tonight?

B. Sure. What would you like to see?

A. **How about**[1] *The Missing Jewels*?

B. *The Missing Jewels*?

A. Yes. It's playing at the Paramount Theater.

B. What's it about?

A. I don't know. The ad in the paper says, "You'll never guess who did it!"

B. Hmm. Sounds like a mystery.* Who's in it?

A. Peter Winston and Jessica Lane. Are you interested?

B. Sure. What time is it showing?

A. **Let's see.**[2] There are shows at 7:10 and 9:25.

B. I think **I'd prefer to**[3] go at 7:10. Is that okay?

A. Sure. That sounds fine to me.

[1] What about

[2] Let me see.

[3] I'd rather

mystery
7:10/9:25

1 adventure movie
7:30/9:45

2 drama
eight/ten

3 comedy
6:40/8:35

Make plans to see a movie tonight.

* mystery
comedy
drama
documentary
western
adventure movie
cartoon
children's film
foreign film
science fiction movie

Movie Match

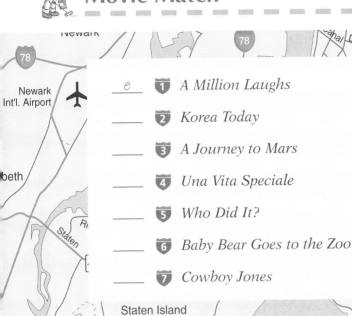

_e_	**1**	*A Million Laughs*	a.	a western
___	**2**	*Korea Today*	b.	a mystery
___	**3**	*A Journey to Mars*	c.	a documentary
___	**4**	*Una Vita Speciale*	d.	a children's film
___	**5**	*Who Did It?*	e.	a comedy
___	**6**	*Baby Bear Goes to the Zoo*	f.	a science fiction movie
___	**7**	*Cowboy Jones*	g.	a foreign film

Listen

Listen to the movie theater recordings and answer the questions.

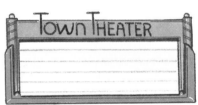

1 The first show is at ___.
   a. 6:45
   b. 7:30

2 There are ___ shows.
   a. three
   b. two

3 Each ticket costs ___.
   a. $7.00
   b. $11.00

4 The name of the movie is ___.
   a. *We Are Happy*
   b. *The Friendly Giant*

5 They show the movie ___ a day.
   a. once
   b. three times

6 The tickets for the 5:00 show are ___ each.
   a. $6.00
   b. $3.00

Community Connections

Look in your local newspaper and find a movie you're interested in seeing.

Call the theater to find out what time the movie starts.

Invite another student in your class to see the movie with you.

See the movie. How was it?

Tell the class about it.

INTERCHANGE

What Do You Want to Watch?

A. What do you want to watch?

B. I don't know. What's on?

A. Well, *Dr. Goodbody* is on Channel 2.

B. Oh, I'd rather not watch *Dr. Goodbody*. I'm tired of watching that program. What else is on?

A. Well, there's a new situation comedy* on Channel 4.

B. I'm not really in the mood for a situation comedy. Are you?

A. No, I guess not. How about *Million Dollar Jackpot* on Channel 5?

B. *Million Dollar Jackpot*? What's that? A game show?

A. I'm not sure. It doesn't say in the TV listings, but it probably is. Do you want to watch it?

B. I don't think so. Is there anything else to watch?

A. Let's see. How about watching *Pittsburgh Police* on Channel 7? That's supposed to be a pretty good show.

B. *Pittsburgh Police*? I don't know. Maybe we should watch *Dr. Goodbody* after all.

A. It doesn't make any difference to me.

B. Are you sure?

A. Yes. Whatever you'd like to watch is fine with me.

*situation comedy   police show
game show   children's show
drama   soap opera
detective show   miniseries

A. What do you want to watch?

B. I don't know. What's on?

A. Well, _____ is on Channel _____.

B. Oh, I'd rather not watch _____. I'm tired of watching that program. What else is on?

A. Well, there's a new _____* on Channel _____.

B. I'm not really in the mood for a _____.* Are you?

A. No, I guess not. How about _____ on Channel _____?

B. _____? What's that? A _____?*

A. I'm not sure. It doesn't say in the TV listings, but it probably is. Do you want to watch it?

B. I don't think so. Is there anything else to watch?

A. Let's see. How about watching _____ on Channel _____? That's supposed to be a pretty good show.

B. _____? I don't know. Maybe we should watch _____ after all.

A. It doesn't make any difference to me.

B. Are you sure?

A. Yes. Whatever you'd like to watch is fine with me.

You can't decide what to watch on TV. Create an original conversation, using the model dialog above as a guide. Feel free to adapt and expand the model any way you wish.

REFLECTIONS
Do you think people watch too much TV? What are some good things and some bad things about television? What effect does television have on young children?

Discuss in pairs or small groups, and then share your ideas with the class.

Television Match

_f_ **1**	I'm not in the mood to watch a situation _____.	a. 8:00
_____ **2**	I'd rather watch a game _____.	b. opera
_____ **3**	I'm tired of watching that soap _____.	c. TV listings
_____ **4**	What's on _____?	d. show
_____ **5**	What's on at _____?	e. Channel 7
_____ **6**	Let's look in the _____.	f. comedy

SAN FRANCISCO

Cow Palace

Oakland International

Lake Chabot

880

35

1

101

Game Refuge

Fremont

The way that people all over the world watch movies has changed in recent years. People don't just go to the movies anymore. They take the movie home! The videocassette recorder, or VCR, has made this possible, and it has helped change people's lives.

Going to movie theaters can be enjoyable, but sometimes it isn't a very pleasant experience. People have to stand in line to buy tickets, which might cost seven dollars or more apiece. Several more dollars are spent on popcorn, candy, and drinks. Sometimes it's difficult to find good seats, and often the seats are uncomfortable. In addition, there is always the possibility that a very tall person will sit down in front of the moviegoer and block the screen. It can also be disturbing when people get up to go to the snack bar or to the bathroom in the middle of the film.

VCRs offer an alternative to a night at the movies. People can simply go to a video store in their neighborhood, rent one or more movies for a day or a weekend, and watch them in the comfort of their own home. Videotapes can also be rented at many supermarkets, drug stores, and convenience stores. They aren't very expensive, just a few dollars per day. Many different movies are available on videotape, from adventure movies and comedies to science fiction films and westerns.

Watching a movie at home can be very convenient, and a lot cheaper. VCR owners can make their own popcorn and other snacks and sit back and enjoy a film with family and friends. They can stop the movie to make more snacks, answer the phone, or check on the baby. There are no lines to stand in, no tickets to buy, and no uncomfortable movie theater seats.

For many people, however, enjoying a movie still means a night out at the neighborhood movie theater. For these moviegoers, nothing can replace the excitement of watching their favorite actors and actresses as they appear larger than life on a big movie screen. And for them, waiting in line, running to get good seats, and sitting with a huge box of popcorn surrounded by other moviegoers is all part of the special movie theater experience that a VCR just can't match.

True or False?

1. VCRs have changed the way people watch movies.
2. VCRs cost just a few dollars.
3. People like the convenience of VCRs.
4. You can only rent videotapes from video stores.
5. Many people still prefer to go to movie theaters.

What's the Answer?

1. When people *disturb* you, they _____.
   a. bother you
   b. make you comfortable
   c. don't bother you at all

2. VCR owners appreciate the fact that _____.
   a. social life has changed
   b. VCRs can be rented
   c. videotapes can be stopped when it's necessary

3. An alternative to watching a video at home is _____.
   a. using a VCR
   b. watching a movie in a theater
   c. renting a video from a video store

4. A VCR is an example of _____.
   a. a video store
   b. the movie industry
   c. modern technology

CrossTalk

How about you? Do you have a VCR?
How often do you rent movies?
What kind of movies do you prefer to rent?
In your opinion, what are the advantages
   of having a VCR?

Or do you prefer to see movies at a movie theater?
What are your favorite kinds of movies?
Who are your favorite movie stars?
What are the advantages of watching movies
   in a movie theater?

Talk with a partner and then tell the class about your discussion.

Interview

Interview people you know and ask what their preferences are. Do they prefer to watch movies at home on their VCRs, or do they prefer to go to a movie theater? Report your findings to the class.

Making a Suggestion
How about ____ing?
What about ____ing?

How about ____?
What about ____?

Let's ____!
Why don't we ____?

Responding to a Suggestion
Good idea!
Good suggestion!

Preference
I'd prefer to ____.
I'd rather ____.

Want-Desire
I don't really feel like ____ing.
I'm not really in the mood to ____.

Indifference
It doesn't make any difference to me.
It doesn't matter to me.
I don't care.

Inability
I can't.
I won't be able to.

Extending an Invitation
Would you like to ____?
How would you like to ____?
Do you want to ____?
Would you be interested in ____ing?
Would you by any chance be interested in ____ing?

Accepting an Invitation
That sounds great.
That sounds like fun.
I'd love to.
I'd like to.

Obligation
I have to ____.
I've got to ____.
I'm supposed to ____.

Regret
That's a shame!
That's too bad!
What a shame!
What a pity!

Hesitating
Let's see.
Let me see.

Now Leaving Exit 8 Construction Area

- Gerunds/Infinitives
- Review: Present Perfect Tense
- Past Perfect Tense
- Past Perfect Continuous Tense

Sorry for the inconvenience. For more information see pages 170 and 171.

ExpressWays Checklist
I can . . .
- Make plans with people
- Discuss recreation preferences
- Extend invitations
- Decline invitations
- Tell about past weekend activities
- Tell about travel and recreation experiences
- Use the newspaper to make movie plans
- Discuss television preferences

REST STOP

Take a break!
Have a conversation!

Here are some scenes from Exits 7 and 8.

Who do you think these people are?
What do you think they're talking about?

In pairs or small groups, create conversations based on these scenes and act them out.

Appendix

- **Grammar Constructions**
- **Cardinal Numbers**
- **Ordinal Numbers**
- **Irregular Verbs**
- **Scripts for Listening Exercises**
- **Grammar Index**
- **Topic Index**

Exit 1 Constructions

Simple Present Tense

Which apartment **do** you live in?
Where **are** you from?
I **have** a reservation.
I **don't** remember.

Present Continuous Tense

What **are** you major**ing** in?
You**'re** stay**ing** 3 nights.

Past Tense

When **did** you move in?
I **requested** a king-size bed.
I **left** my membership card at home.

Future: Will

Somebody **will** see you in a few minutes.

WH-Questions

Who is your supervisor?
What are you majoring in?
When did you move in?
Where are you from?
Why are you here?
Which apartment do you live in?
Whose English class are you in?
How are you enjoying your work?

Question Formation

Am I?	Is	he she ? it	Are	we you ? they
Do	I we ? you they		Does	he she ? it

Exit 2 Constructions

Yes/No Questions

Is our English teacher going to quit?
Are they going to lay off the workers?
Do the bus drivers plan to go on strike?
Does our supervisor want to shorten our
    coffee break?
Did the boss fire Fred?
Was our gym teacher in the 1992 Olympics?

Negative Sentences

Our English teacher **isn't** going to quit.
They **aren't** going to lay off the workers.
The bus drivers **don't** plan to go on strike.
Our supervisor **doesn't** want to shorten our
    coffee break.
The boss **didn't** fire Fred.
Our gym teacher **wasn't** in the 1992 Olympics.

Question Formation

What do you want to know?
Where are you from?

Are you originally from around here?
Do you have any brothers and sisters?

Past Tense

I just **passed** my driver's test!
I just **got** a big promotion!
My wife **had** a baby girl last week!
My husband and I **won** the state lottery!
My daughter **broke up** with her fiancé!

You **did**?
You **didn't**?

I **didn't** get the raise!

Future: Going to

Our English teacher is **going to** quit.

Future: Will

I'll probably visit my grandchildren.

Exit 3 Constructions

Question Formation

How do you spell that?
Where can I get the 8:30 flight to Chicago?
When is the next flight?

Are you sure you have the correct address?
Would you like to puchase a ticket?
Will that get you to Chicago in time?

Negative Sentences

I **don't** have a Carlos Ramirez
on Beach Boulevard.

No, it **isn't**.
No, it **doesn't**.

Simple Present Tense

Does this train go to the Bronx?
No, it **doesn't**.

It **goes** to Queens.

Past Tense

I **dialed** the wrong number.
I **turned** right.
I **went** north on Union Boulevard.
I **drove** to Washington Avenue.
I **took** the parkway south and **got off** at Exit 14.

You **were** supposed to get off at Exit 15.

Imperatives

Go to the next corner.
Walk three blocks to Second Avenue and **turn** right.

Have to/Have Got to

I **have to** get to my brother's wedding.
I**'ve got to** get to my brother's wedding.

Exit 4 Constructions

Adjectives

It's very **safe**.
It has a **brand new** refrigerator.
We're looking for a **two-bedroom** apartment.
These are **delicious.**
They're a **popular Mexican** dish.

Singular/Plural

It has a brand new refrigerator.
You don't find many two-bedroom apartments
    with brand new refrigerator**s.**

Count Nouns

We need **a few** oranges.
How **many**?

Lamb chop**s**?
They're in the Frozen Food Section.

The vitamins **were** six ninety-four.

These are delicious! What **are they?**
They're enchiladas.
What's in **them**?
A few tomatoes.

Non-Count Nouns

We need **some** sugar.
How **much**?

Yogurt?
It's in the Dairy Section.

The skim milk **was** a dollar seventeen.

This is excellent! What **is it**?
It's borscht.
What's in **it**?
A little water.

Partitives

a bag of sugar
a bottle of mineral water
a box of rice
a bunch of bananas
a can of tuna fish
a container of yogurt
a dozen eggs
a gallon of milk
a head of lettuce
a jar of peanut butter
a loaf of bread
a pint of ice cream
a pound of coffee
a quart of orange juice
a six-pack of soda
a stick of butter
a tube of toothpaste
half a dozen eggs
half a pound of Swiss cheese
a half gallon of milk
a pound and a half of ground beef

a cup of bread crumbs
half a cup of milk
a teaspoon of salt

Pronouns

What are **they**?
They're enchiladas.
What's in **them**?

What is **it**?
It's borscht.
What's in **it**?

Imperatives

Mix together one egg, two teaspoons of salt,
and two pounds of ground beef.

Exit 5 Constructions

Present Perfect Tense

(I have) (We have) (You have) (They have)	I've We've You've They've	
		eaten.
(He has) (She has) (It has)	He's She's It's	

Have	I we you they	
		eaten?
Has	he she it	

	I we you they	have.
Yes,		
	he she it	has.

	I we you they	haven't.
No,		
	he she it	hasn't.

Since/For

I've known	**for** many years. five years. the past few years. *[period of time]*	**since** 1994. last year. I came to this country. *[point in time]*

Present Perfect Continuous Tense

(I have) (We have) (You have) (They have)	I've We've You've They've	been living here since 1990.
(He has) (She has) (It has)	He's She's It's	

Contrast: Present Perfect, Present Perfect Continuous, and Past Tenses

The bookkeeper's primary responsibility is to **oversee** the company's finances.
I**'ve been overseeing** the company's finances for years.

In addition, the bookkeeper **does** the payroll.
I **haven't done** the payroll in my current position.
I **did** the payroll in the job I had before that.

Past Continuous to Express Future Intention

I **was planning to** give them out this afternoon.
I **was going to** give them out this afternoon.

Exit 6 Constructions

Present Perfect Tense

A tour bus **has overturned**.
Someone **has** just **broken into** my house.

Have you ever **been** hospitalized?
   No, I **haven't**.
How long **have** you **had** a migraine headache?

How long **hasn't** he **been able** to move his neck?

Since/For

How long have you had a bad toothache?
   Since Sunday morning.

How long have you had a migraine headache?
   For two days.

Present Perfect Continuous Tense

How long **have** you **been feeling** dizzy?
How long **has** your right ear **been ringing**?

Prepositions of Location

At the corner of Maple and B Street.
At the intersection of Harrison Road and 30th Street.
Across the street from Charlie's Café.
On the north side of Crystal Pond.
In front of the Save-Rite Store on Fifth Street.
Near Exit 17.

It's **in** Aisle 3 **on** the right.
It's **in** Aisle 2 **halfway down on** the left.
It's **on** the top shelf **next to** the toothpaste.
It's **in** the last aisle **on** the bottom shelf.
It's **in** the Cold Medicine section.
It's **in** the front of the store **near** the checkout counter.

Question Formation

Do you have any allergies?
Are you on a special diet of any kind?
Have you ever been hospitalized?

Supposed to

I'm He's She's It's We're You're They're	**supposed to** do that.

Exit 7 Constructions

Prepositions of Location

They're **in** the Houshold Appliances Department **in** the basement.
They're **on** the second floor.
You'll see Children's Clothing **on** the left.
You'll see Furniture **on** the right **in** the corner.
They're **at** the rear of the store.
There's an elevator **near** the main entrance.
Walk **up** this staircase.
Walk **down** this aisle **past** Women's Clothing.

Adjectives

I'm looking for a **leather** belt.
A **size 36 dark brown leather** belt.
It's too **lightweight**.
They're too **long**.

Too

It's **too** lightweight.
They're **too** long.

Comparatives

Would you like to exchange them
for some **shorter** ones?
heavier
bigger
larger
more difficult

One/Ones

Which **one** are you interested in?
   I'd like the **one** with the 25-inch screen.
Would you like to exchange it for a heavier **one**?

Would you like to exchange them for some shorter **ones**?

Future: Will

How long **will** that take?
That**'ll** cost five ninety-four.
I**'ll** send it parcel post.

Singular/Plural

I'd like to purchase a money order.
Money order**s** can be purchased at Window Number 3.

Passives: Introduction

Money orders can **be purchased** at Window Number 3.
Registered letters can **be sent** at the next window.

Exit 8 Constructions

Gerunds/Infinitives	
I don't want to	**play** tennis. **go** to the movies. **have** a picnic.
I don't feel like	**playing** tennis. **going** to the movies. **having** a picnic.

Going skiing wouldn't be a very good idea.
Going dancing sounds like a lot more fun than **working** overtime.

I'd prefer **to go** to the town pool.

Review: Present Perfect Tense
I **haven't gone** skiing in a long time. We **haven't seen** a movie in a long time.

Past Perfect Tense

I He She It We You They	had/hadn't	gone.

Past Perfect Continous Tense

I He She It We You They	had been working.

CARDINAL NUMBERS

1	one	20	twenty
2	two	21	twenty-one
3	three	22	twenty-two
4	four	.	
5	five	.	
6	six	29	twenty-nine
7	seven	30	thirty
8	eight	40	forty
9	nine	50	fifty
10	ten	60	sixty
11	eleven	70	seventy
12	twelve	80	eighty
13	thirteen	90	ninety
14	fourteen	100	one hundred
15	fifteen	200	two hundred
16	sixteen	300	three hundred
17	seventeen	.	
18	eighteen	.	
19	nineteen	900	nine hundred
		1,000	one thousand
		2,000	two thousand
		3,000	three thousand
		.	
		.	
		10,000	ten thousand
		100,000	one hundred thousand
		1,000,000	one million

ORDINAL NUMBERS

1st	first	20th	twentieth
2nd	second	21st	twenty-first
3rd	third	22nd	twenty-second
4th	fourth	.	
5th	fifth	.	
6th	sixth	29th	twenty-ninth
7th	seventh	30th	thirtieth
8th	eighth	40th	fortieth
9th	ninth	50th	fiftieth
10th	tenth	60th	sixtieth
11th	eleventh	70th	seventieth
12th	twelfth	80th	eightieth
13th	thirteenth	90th	ninetieth
14th	fourteenth	100th	one hundredth
15th	fifteenth		
16th	sixteenth	1,000th	one thousandth
17th	seventeenth	1,000,000th	one millionth
18th	eighteenth		
19th	nineteenth		

IRREGULAR VERBS

be	was/were	been
begin	began	begun
break	broke	broken
bring	brought	brought
build	built	built
buy	bought	bought
catch	caught	caught
come	came	come
cut	cut	cut
do	did	done
draw	drew	drawn
drive	drove	driven
eat	ate	eaten
fall	fell	fallen
feed	fed	fed
feel	felt	felt
find	found	found
fly	flew	flown
forget	forgot	forgotten
get	got	gotten
give	gave	given
go	went	gone
grow	grew	grown
hang	hung	hung
have	had	had
hear	heard	heard
hit	hit	hit
hold	held	held
hurt	hurt	hurt
keep	kept	kept
know	knew	known
leave	left	left
lend	lent	lent
let	let	let
lose	lost	lost

make	made	made
mean	meant	meant
meet	met	met
put	put	put
read	read	read
ride	rode	ridden
ring	rang	rung
run	ran	run
say	said	said
see	saw	seen
sell	sold	sold
send	sent	sent
set	set	set
show	showed	shown
sing	sang	sung
sit	sat	sat
sleep	slept	slept
speak	spoke	spoken
speed	sped	sped
spend	spent	spent
stand	stood	stood
steal	stole	stolen
sweep	swept	swept
swim	swam	swum
take	took	taken
teach	taught	taught
tell	told	told
think	thought	thought
throw	threw	thrown
understand	understood	understood
wake	woke	woken
wear	wore	worn
win	won	won
write	wrote	written

SCRIPTS FOR LISTENING EXERCISES

Page 5

Listen and choose the right answer.

1. Where's Michael?
2. Who are you?
3. When did you move in?
4. Where are you going?
5. How's Janet?
6. Which apartment do you live in?
7. What are you majoring in?
8. My name is Elsa.
9. How do you do?

Page 23

Listen and choose the most appropriate response.

1. I got the raise I was hoping for!
2. My husband wrecked our car last weekend!
3. My daughter broke up with her fiancé last week.
4. My wife got a big promotion!
5. Our next-door neighbor's apartment was robbed last night!
6. I'm really enjoying my classes.
7. I didn't pass my driver's test.
8. I had a wonderful time on my vacation.
9. My wife had a baby last night!

Page 31

Listen and choose the correct answer.

1. A. Are you from Los Angeles?
   B. No, I'm from Denver.

2. A. What do you do?
   B. I'm a gym teacher.

3. A. I'm going to get a raise!
   B. Me, too!

4. A. I just passed my driver's test!
   B. Congratulations!

5. A. So, what's new?
   B. All my employees plan to go on strike soon.

6. A. Is Fred going to quit?
   B. Not as far as I know.

7. A. What did you do in Vancouver?
   B. I went to college there.

8. A. Where are you from?
   B. I was born in Taipei and lived there until I finished high school.

9. A. What did you do in England?
   B. I was a journalist.

10. A. Do you have any children?
    B. Yes. I have a boy and a girl.

Page 37

Listen 1

Listen and complete the sentence.

1. My friend is living . . .
2. Did he stop . . . ?
3. Please . . .
4. I put the cars . . .
5. Let's work . . .
6. Did you take him . . . ?
7. Do you have any plans . . . ?
8. Let's clean the kitchen . . .
9. Do you know who . . . ?

176

Listen 2

Listen to the conversation and circle the word you hear.

1. A. I'd like the number of David Yu.
   B. How do you spell that?
   A. Y-U.

2. A. How do you spell Flanigan?
   B. F-L-A-N-I-G-A-N.

3. A. What street?
   B. Beech Road.
   A. B-E-E-C-H?
   B. Yes.

4. A. Can you spell that?
   B. Sure. W-I-T-T-L-E-R.

5. Just a moment. I'd better check the spelling. Yes, it's K-R-I-Z-I-C-K.

6. A. How do you spell Rio de Janeiro?
   B. R-I-O D-E J-A-N-E-I-R-O.

7. A. Did you say H-E-N-L-E-Y?
   B. Yes.

8. A. Do you spell Ramirez with a "z" or an "s"?
   B. With a "z."

Page 39

Listen to the conversation and choose the number you hear.

1. A. I'd like the number of Bob Williams.
   B. Just a moment. The number is 539-7899.

2. A. Is this 592-8622?
   B. Yes, it is.

3. A. I guess I dialed the wrong number.
   B. What number did you dial?
   A. 832-5660.

4. A. Did you dial 860-5439?
   B. Yes, I did.

5. A. What's your telephone number?
   B. 834-5935.

6. A. Are you sure this is the correct number?
   B. Let me check. 648-2341. Yes, that's it.

Page 43

Listen to the announcements. Which words do you hear?

1. The bus for Las Vegas is now leaving from gate thirteen.
2. Attention . . . passengers for New York and New Haven . . . your bus is at gate eleven.
3. Attention, passengers. The nine-thirty bus is now boarding at gate five.
4. Your attention, please. The three o'clock bus to Philadelphia is now boarding.
5. Attention, please. The eleven forty-five bus to Kansas City is now leaving from gate seventeen.
6. Attention . . . passengers for San Francisco. Your bus is now boarding at gate twelve.
7. Passengers going to Chicago . . . Your bus will leave at ten thirty from gate two.
8. Your attention, please. The next bus to Baltimore will leave from gate eight.

Page 46

Listen and follow the directions to different places. Write the letter of the place people are talking about in each conversation.

1. A. Excuse me. Could you please tell me how to get to the library?
   B. Okay. Walk down Fourth Street to Broad Street and turn left. Walk one block, and you'll see the library on the corner of Third and Broad.
   A. Thanks.

2. A. Can you tell me how to get to the laundromat?
   B. Sure. Walk down Oak Street to Third Street and make a right. You'll see the laundromat in the middle of the block.
   A. Thanks very much.

3. A. Excuse me. How do I get to the zoo?
   B. Follow Fourth Street to Broad Street. Make a left on Broad Street and go three more blocks to First Street. You'll see the zoo on the left, at the intersection of First and Broad.
   A. Thanks very much.

4. A. Pardon me. Do you know how to get to Max's Supermarket?
   B. Uh-húh. Follow Fourth Street all the way to the end and make a left. Go one block, and you'll see it on the left.
   A. Thank you.

5. A. Excuse me. Could you possibly tell me how to get to River City High School?
   B. Uh-húh. Go down Fourth Street two blocks and make a left onto Broad Street. Go two more blocks and make a right on Second Street. You'll see the school on your right.
   A. Thank you very much.

6. A. Excuse me. Is there a parking lot nearby?
   B. Yes. Follow Fourth Street all the way to the end. You'll see it on the left.
   A. Thanks.

7. A. Pardon me. Where's City Hall?
   B. Follow Oak Street two blocks and make a right onto Second Street. Walk two more blocks, and you'll see City Hall at the intersection of Broad and Second.
   A. Thanks very much.

8. A. I'm looking for the bus station. Can you help me?
   B. Sure. Walk down Fourth Street and make a left on Main Street. Follow Main Street to Second Street. You'll see the bus station on the left.
   A. Thank you.

9. A. Pardon me. Do you by any chance know where the bank is?
   B. Yes. Go down Fourth to Main and make a left. Go two blocks and make a right. The bank is in the middle of the block on the right.
   A. Thank you very much.

Page 47

Listen to the conversation. Did the person understand the directions?

1. A. Take Exit 15.
   B. I'm following you.

2. A. Go north.
   B. Could you please repeat that?

3. A. Turn left at Second Avenue.
   B. I didn't get that.

4. A. Take the first right, and you'll see a sign.
   B. I understand.

5. A. Go to the next corner and turn right.
   B. I didn't follow you.

6. A. Drive through three traffic lights and make a right.
   B. I'm with you.

7. A. Turn left at the light, go about a mile, and you'll see a sign.
   B. I've got it.

8. A. Take the second left after the intersection.
   B. All right.

9. A. Take a right and go about seven blocks.
   B. I didn't get that.

Page 63

Listen and complete the sentence.

1. I need a dozen . . .
2. Could you pick up a quart of . . . ?
3. We have to get a jar of . . .
4. Did you get a tube of . . . ?
5. Can you do me a favor and get a box of . . . ?
6. I've got to get a head of . . .
7. I need a stick of . . .
8. Could you buy a few . . . ?

Listen and choose the letter or number you hear.

1. Excuse me. Did you say Aisle 3?
2. Sorry. Did you say H Street?
3. Is this Aisle J?
4. You can find it in Aisle 8.
5. Do you spell that with a D?
6. I'm sorry. I said G.
7. We need fourteen.
8. Pardon me. Is this N Street?
9. What number is this? Seventy?
10. Sorry. Did you say Aisle F?

What prices do you hear?

1. That comes to thirteen dollars and fifteen cents.
2. The total is eighteen dollars and ten cents.
3. Your change is seven dollars and forty cents.
4. It's hard to believe how little you can buy for sixteen dollars and forty-three cents.
5. Fifteen dollars and seventy-six cents? That's unbelievable!
6. How about that! It's only thirty dollars and fifty-eight cents.
7. That'll be twenty-two dollars and eleven cents.
8. Nineteen dollars and eighty-eight cents, please.
9. Nine dollars and ninety-eight cents? That's cheap!

Listen and decide what the people are talking about.

1. These aren't difficult to make.
2. It's really delicious!

3. I think it's really convenient.
4. It has a brand new kitchen.
5. It's very complicated.
6. It's within walking distance of the school.

Listen and put a check next to the task that each employee has already done and an ✗ next to the task that the employee hasn't done yet.

1. A. Howard, have you typed those letters yet?
   B. Yes, I have, Mrs. Johnson. I typed them this afternoon.
   A. That's good. And have you also made copies of them?
   B. No, I haven't made the copies yet. I'll do that in a few minutes.
   A. Oh, and one more thing, Howard. Have you gotten the mail from the mailroom yet?
   B. Not yet, Mrs. Johnson. I'll get the mail right after I make the copies of the letters.
   A. That's fine. Oh, and before I forget, Howard. You need to speak to Mr. Chen in Personnel about changing your work schedule for next month.
   B. I've already spoken with him, and everything has been arranged.

2. A. Stella, have you fixed the copy machine yet? It's been broken for over a week.
   B. I've already fixed it, Mr. Leonard. I fixed it early this morning.
   A. That's great. And have you cleaned the supply room yet?
   B. Not yet. I'll do that later this morning, after I go to the post office.
   A. Oh, by the way, Stella. I noticed that you haven't filled out your time sheet for this week.
   B. I'm sorry, Mr. Leonard. I'll do it right away.

3. A. Mrs. Giannini, I've already set the tables, I've put the glasses out, and I've arranged all the flowers.
   B. That's wonderful, Richard. I guess we're all ready for tonight. By the way, have you vacuumed the floor yet? It really needs to be done.
   A. Sorry, Mrs. Giannini. I'll vacuum it right away.
   B. Thanks, Richard.

4. A. I'm sorry I haven't written that report yet, Mr. Davis. I'll write it over the weekend.
   B. No problem, Richard.
   A. And I'm also sorry I haven't given out the paychecks yet, Mr. Davis. I'll give them out right away.
   B. Please do that, Richard. The paychecks are supposed to be given out right after lunch.
   A. Oh, that reminds me, Mr. Davis. I haven't eaten lunch yet.
   B. Richard. Have you met with your supervisor recently?
   A. You mean Mr. Cooper? No, I haven't. I haven't met with him in a long time.
   B. Richard, I think there are a few things you need to talk to Mr. Cooper about . . . as soon as possible!
   A. Of course, Mr. Davis. I'll speak to him right away . . . after I eat lunch.

5. A. Shirley, the animals seem to be very hungry today. Have you fed them yet?
   B. Yes, I have. I fed them a few minutes ago. And I also cleaned all the cages.
   A. You did? That's great. By the way, Shirley, you were going to repair the van. It really needs to be fixed.
   B. No, problem, Mr. Miller. I'll repair it in a little while.
   A. One last thing, Shirley. Have you walked Mrs. Carter's dog? Remember, you're supposed to walk him a few times a day.
   B. I've already walked him twice today, Mr. Miller, but I'll walk him again if you want me to.
   A. No, that's fine. Twice is enough.

6. A. Mrs. Hernandez, I've made all the beds and I've polished the tables in the lobby.
   B. That's wonderful, Emily. Now you need to wash the uniforms.
   A. I've already washed them, Mrs. Hernandez.
   B. You have? That's great.
   A. Yes, I washed them all this morning.
   B. By the way, Emily. Do you know that we have several new rules and regulations for employees here at the Royal Plaza Hotel?
   A. Yes, I know, Mrs. Hernandez. I've already read them all.

Page 89

Listen and choose the correct answer.

1. Roger took violin lessons for five years.
2. My daughter has been studying Spanish for two years.
3. Mark was an architect.
4. My children have known how to ski for a long time.
5. Elena has been a computer programmer since college.
6. I've been working in the Accounting Department for a long time.
7. Irene was a receptionist until the office shut down.
8. The truth is, I haven't been happy in my job for a long time.

Page 95

Listen and choose the correct conclusion.

1. Could you please send an engine unit right away?
2. I think there's a robber in my neighbor's house!
3. Call the animal removal specialist right away!
4. The kitchen floor has flooded!
5. Please send an ambulance right away!
6. Can you send a squad car?

Listen to the conversation and then answer true or false.

A. Police.

B. I want to report an accident.

A. Okay.

B. An airplane has landed on the expressway.

A. What's your name?

B. Rick Walters.

A. Where did this occur?

B. About two miles south of the airport, near Exit 4.

A. Okay. We'll be there right away.

    1. There was an accident at the airport.
    2. Rick Walters called to report the accident.

Now listen to the next conversation.

A. Police.

B. I want to report a robbery.

A. Okay. Go ahead.

B. A drug store has just been robbed at Milford Shopping Mall.

A. What's your name?

B. Helen Nichols.

    3. Helen Milford called to report a robbery.
    4. Someone robbed a drug store.

Now listen to the next conversation.

A. Sergeant Garner.

B. I'd like to report a mugging.

A. Yes. Go on.

B. A man just mugged two women in front of my apartment building. The address is forty-two fifty-three Harrison Street.

    5. Two women just mugged someone.
    6. Sergeant Garner called to report the mugging.

Now listen to the next conversation.

A. Police Department.

B. There's been an accident on Highway 85. A patrol car has been hit by a bus.

    7. An accident has just occurred on Highway 85.
    8. A police car and a bus were in an accident.

Listen and decide what each person's problem is.

1. Can you suggest a good lotion?
2. I recommend this new decongestant spray.
3. I need a couple of aspirin.
4. It gets frizzy in this humidity.
5. Try these eyedrops.
6. I didn't sleep well last night.

Listen and complete the sentence.

1. I parked the car near . . .
2. Take the elevator to . . .
3. Household appliances? They're on . . .
4. We left it at the front of the . . .
5. Did they put the boxes in . . .?
6. The staircase is on the . . .

Listen to the conversation. What are these people talking about?

1. A. Which one are you interested in?
    B. The one with the 18-inch screen.

2. A. Which one would you like?
    B. The one that beeps every hour.

3. A. Which one would you like to buy?
    B. The one with two doors.

4. A. Which one would you like to try?
    B. The one with a manual transmission.

5. A. Which one should we buy?
   B. The one that's on sale.

6. A. Which one do you want?
   B. The one with the largest memory.

7. A. Which one should we buy?
   B. The one with remote control.

8. A. Which one did you get?
   B. The self-cleaning one.

Page 121

Listen to the conversation. What word do you hear?

1. A. I'm looking for a brown leather belt.
   B. What size?
   A. 34.

2. A. Do you know what size you are?
   B. Yes. I'm a 15 neck and a 33 sleeve.
   A. All right. One moment, please.

3. A. Which one do you like?
   B. The blue one.

4. A. I'd like this skirt in a medium.
   B. Yes. Here you are.

5. A. I usually wear a size 7.
   B. Here. Try this in a small.

6. A. Which one will you take?
   B. I'll take the red and white one.

7. A. I'll take this brown one.
   B. Okay. Will this be cash or charge?

8. A. I'd like to buy a blue permanent press blouse.
   B. What size?
   A. Twelve, I think.

9. A. Do you think your brother will like this coat?
   B. Yes. Definitely. I'll take it.

10. A. I want to buy a beige belt . . . size 32.
    B. All right. Let's look on that rack over there.

11. A. Do you have this shirt in a permanent press?
    B. Yes, we do.

12. A. Will this be cash?
    B. No. I'll pay with my MasterCard.

Page 123

Listen and choose the best answer.

1. Could you carry this box for me?
2. This recipe is very simple.
3. You know, we need a larger rug.
4. These earrings are too tight!
5. This tie is too conservative!
6. It's too short!
7. Hmm. This brown belt is too dark!
8. I had trouble with this exercise!

Page 129

Listen and choose the correct number.

1. A. How long will it take?
   B. It'll take about ten days.

2. A. How much will it cost?
   B. It'll be twelve dollars and ninety-six cents.

3. A. How much does it weigh?
   B. It's eleven pounds.

4. A. What's the cost?
   B. Fourteen sixty-eight.

5. A. When will it get there?
   B. It'll get there in about nine days.

6. A. How heavy is it?
   B. Four pounds.

7. A. How much will that be?
   B. It'll be thirteen seventy-eight.

8. A. How much do I owe you?
   B. Twelve sixty-four.

Page 139

Listen and decide which weather forecast is correct.

1. Here's today's weather forecast for the metropolitan area. We're going to have rain this afternoon. Temperatures will be in the low eighties.

2. Here is the weather update for our area. We have a sunny day ahead. The present temperature is forty-five degrees. Tonight's low will be in the thirties.

3. A. And now, let's hear the weather report from Jim Reed.
   B. Thank you, Jane. It looks like we'll have a little snow this morning . . . but nothing to worry about. And put on those heavy jackets! Today's high will be only about twenty-five.

4. It's going to be a hot, muggy evening with temperatures in the mid-eighties. We have a seventy percent chance of thunderstorms throughout the night.

5. Now here's our latest weather update from Rockin' Ninety-Nine Weather Center. The good news is NO MORE RAIN in the forecast. We'll have clearing tonight, but watch out for fog early tomorrow morning while you're driving to work.

6. A. Now it's time to hear from our weather reporter, Mike Martinez. Mike, what does it look like out there today?
   B. Well, Susan, hold on to your hat! We're in for a windy day with gusts up to twenty miles per hour.

Page 141

Listen and decide whether someone accepted or rejected the other person's invitation.

1. A. Carol, how about going out for dinner tonight?
   B. Tonight? That sounds great.

2. A. Bob, do you want to go bowling tomorrow night?
   B. Tomorrow night? I'm afraid I can't. I've got to baby-sit for my cousin.

3. A. Angela, how would you like to see a ballgame with me this weekend?
   B. I'd love to.

4. A. Lucy, would you by any chance be interested in going to a movie with me this Friday night?
   B. This Friday night? Hmm. Let me think. You know, I think I have to help my parents clean the attic. Maybe some other time, Ronald.

5. A. Howard, what about going to a museum with me tomorrow?
   B. Gee, Irene, I'm afraid I won't be able to.
   A. You won't?
   B. No. I've got to finish an important term paper.
   A. Oh.
   B. Maybe some other time, okay?
   A. Sure, Howard.

6. A. Tim, do you feel like going skating this afternoon?
   B. This afternoon? Sure. That's a great idea. I really should do my homework, but I'd much rather go skating with you.

7. A. Millie, let's get together this weekend.
   B. Great idea. What do you want to do?
   A. Let's take a nice long walk in the park.
   B. Okay. When?
   A. How about Sunday afternoon?
   B. Sunday afternoon? Gee, I won't be able to. I've got to work on my taxes this Sunday. Maybe some other time.

8. A. How would you like to play tennis with me this Tuesday afternoon?
   B. This Tuesday? Gee, I think I'm supposed to attend a meeting this Tuesday. No, wait a minute! The meeting is Thursday. Sure. I'd love to play tennis with you on Tuesday.

Listen to the movie theater recordings and
answer the questions.

The **State Theater** is proud to present
One Last Kiss. There are shows this
evening at seven-thirty and nine-thirty.
Tickets are seven dollars apiece.

Thanks for calling the Town Theater.
We're happy to be showing the popular film
The Friendly Giant. The afternoon show is at
one o'clock. Other shows are at three o'clock
and five o'clock. Tickets for the one o'clock
show are three dollars. All other shows are six
dollars each.

GRAMMAR INDEX

TOPIC INDEX